D1825716

Unto The Third And Fourth Generation: A Study

Helen Campbell

UNTO THE

Third and Fourth Generation.

A STUDY.

By HELEN CAMPBELL,

Author of "The Ainslee Series," "His Grandmothers,"
"Chips from a North Western Log," etc.

NEW YORK:
FORDS, HOWARD, & HULBERT.
1880.

———◆———

" Before Man parted for this earthly strand,
    While yet upon the verge of Heaven he stood,
God put a heap of letters in his hand
    And bade him make with them what word he could."

MATTHEW ARNOLD.

———◆———

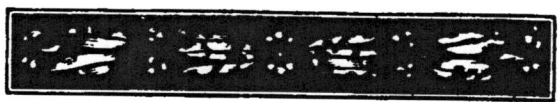

UNTO THE THIRD AND FOURTH GENERATION.

CHAPTER I.

ILAS! Wake up! Silas! There was a knock on the window, just as sure's you're alive. I've heard it three times now."

"If you hadn't been hearin' knocks for thirty years, Huldy, I'd think more of this one," returned Uncle Silas Mann, struggling out of his first heavy sleep. And he sat up to listen, as patiently as if it were part of the night's duty to account for what thus far had been only the nervousness of a timid woman, intensified by years of green tea and stimulated by all the creakings and groanings and unaccountable sounds to which an old house gives itself up at night. "How you're ever goin' to make up all the sleep you've lost keepin' one ear open for nothin', I don't see, Huldy. Do try and get a nap."

Uncle Silas turned over, but as he turned started up again. An unmistakable rap sounded on the win-

dow near the head of the bed, and Aunt Huldy gave
a faint little scream.

"There, Silas! I told you so, an' you wouldn't believe it."

"Who's there? an' what do you want this time o'
night?" Uncle Silas called, as he threw up the window
and peered out.

"Hush—sh!" came softly. "Open the door, still as
you can. I thought you would never hear. Oh, Uncle
Silas!"

Aunt Huldah, whose fears, like those of many timid
women, fled instantly in the presence of any substan-
tial cause, and who had followed her husband at once,
sat down in the high rocking-chair, too overcome by
astonishment to stand.

"For the land's sake! It's Patty Pearsons! Pretty
Patty. For the land's sake!"

Even as she spoke she felt about among her array
of bottles on the little light-stand for matches, and
after much fumbling lighted the candle, which when
Uncle Silas returned cast a faint glimmer on a tall
figure that accompanied him, with pale, set face, and
deep, hollow, dark eyes; a face so full of woe that the
pair looked at it and then at one another aghast.

"'Tain't Patty; it can't be," said Aunt Huldah, and
then checked herself as she saw how the girl trembled.
"You poor lamb, with your hands like ice, and it July
too! Here; crawl right into bed where it's warm, and
I'll start up a fire and make you a good cup o' tea.

You must have a bite o' something before you're fit to say a word."

"I don't want it," came in so despairing a voice that again both started. "I only want Uncle Silas. He was the only one that could help, and nobody here must know. He is the only one. Father tried to keep me from coming; but I had to, and I've walked over from St. Albans Bay to-night. Dunning's sloop brought me there."

"Twelve miles in the dark!" said Aunt Huldah, who never walked save about her house. "No wonder you're white. 'Taint Donald, then. I didn't know but what he'd had a stroke. But, there; don't you speak another word till I've fixed you up something. To think of me askin' a single question an' you lookin' that way!"

Aunt Huldah hurried away to the kitchen, while Uncle Silas took off the light shawl and bonnet, damp with night dews, and laid Patty on the bed as if she had been a baby.

"It's trouble, I know," he said, "an' Uncle Silas 'll stand by ye whatever it is. But half an hour ain't goin' to make it any worse. Jest lie quiet, Patty, an' do as Wife says, an' may the Lord be with you through it."

Patty obeyed, but the strained, eager look in the dark eyes did not alter, and Uncle Silas after a few moments of waiting by her knelt by the bed. What possibilities had entered his mind as he stood there Patty neither knew nor thought, but as his familiar voice sounded in words that seemed instantly to take hold of a helping Presence only waiting this appeal to become visible and potent, she shivered, and shrank away.

"Don't, Uncle Silas," she said. "This isn't a thing we can pray about. If we could I should know better what to do."

"There's nothing so bad that praying can't help it; nothing—" began the old man, but Polly was silent now, and the words seemed checked and to rebound as they left his lips. He rose and again stood by her, waiting for Aunt Huldah, who presently brought in a tray, cleared the light-stand of its burden of camphor bottles and her favorite specifics of one sort and another, and set tea and some tempting food before the girl. At the first mouthful Patty turned away.

"You must," said Uncle Silas imperatively. "Not one word 'll I hear till you've eaten enough to talk on. Don't I tell ye I understand that it's trouble has brought ye? Eat an' you'll tell it better."

Patty obeyed, drinking the tea eagerly and taking a bit of bread. Then she pushed back her heavy hair with a gesture both knew.

"You must get into bed—both of you," she said. "You are shivering, it is so damp. I will sit on the foot, as I used to that year here. I can tell you better so."

The pair obeyed and Patty for a moment was silent.

"I don't know how to tell you," she said with a

groan, "and yet there isn't an hour to lose. Uncle Silas, they've taken up my husband for murder, and he's on trial now for his life."

"She's out of her mind with the walk," said Aunt Huldah faintly. "You hain't got no husband, Patty."

"I hadn't the last time you heard, but I have now. Uncle Silas, it was Robert Saunders after all."

"Tobit Saunders's black sheep?" the old man said mechanically. "Why, Patty, we thought you'd given it up. You never wrote."

"Yes, Tobit Saunders's black sheep," repeated Patty bitterly; "that's what everybody calls him—when there wasn't another such generous, warm-hearted soul in the wilderness. But I never thought you'd say that, Uncle Silas. Handsome and gay and more a gentleman than any of them, and so they'll all be down on him now. They said I was crazy to marry him—I a church member, an' he a man that his own father had turned out because he was wild and wouldn't settle to work. Father nearly turned me out, and he was bound up in me too. You know Father. I'd said 'No' to so many he thought I'd stay by him always—him and Benoni—but Robert followed me up. You know just how he did when he was here. He said he'd go to work any way I liked that wouldn't break us up. He'd burn charcoal, or go into the lumber camp, or get some place about the mines—anything so't I needn't leave Father. Then Father, when he'd found I'd nearly made up my mind, kept the big Bible open day and

night, and the minute Robert came in he'd begin: 'Be
not unequally yoked with an unbeliever; ' and so on,
reading every text he could pick out that went against
us. 'You're the child of prayin' parents, Patty Pearsons,' he said. 'I give you to the Lord in your cradle,
and how 'll I bear it to see you takin' up with a child
o' the devil now? I can't bear it, an' it's killin' me.' I
told him I was a believer an' meant to stay one, but
Robert Saunders had a soul to save as well as other
folks, and he'd a good deal kinder heart to start with
than most. I knew well enough he'd been wild. He
told me the whole, and there wasn't a mean thirg in it;
and he wanted to do better. Oh, Uncle Silas, how
good he was! I didn't know a man could be so tender
and gentle. I never'd seen any one so but you. I was
so happy it seemed as if I couldn't hardly live, and
now I'm punished for it.

"We shouldn't have been married so soon, but one
day we went to the Point and Dunning's sloop was lying there, loading up, and a minister on board going up
to the Gore. Robert said it was all ordered so, and I
didn't make any time because I thought that, once
done, Father would settle down and think there was
no more use in objections. There were two men on
board that stood round and looked sort of curious,
and they asked Robert if he lived there steadily, and
other questions. He didn't make much answer and
was very pale, but I thought that was because of the
strangeness and suddenness of it all; and we were mar-

ried. Then we went home, and he went up to Father and he said very solemnly, 'Mr. Pearsons, I've turned over a new leaf, and I'm going to settle down to work steady, and Patty and I decided not to wait any longer, so we were married this afternoon.' Father didn't speak, and Robert went on, 'I've got nearly three hundred dollars, an' that's more than you had when you started with Patty's mother, for I've heard you say so.'

" 'Where did you get those dollars?' said Father.

" 'I've been saving up,' says Robert, ' ever since I made up my mind to ask for Patty, and you know I sold my colt a month ago.'

" 'If you was a God-fearin' man,' said Father, ' I could stand it if you hadn't a dollar; but, Robert Saunders, you ain't, an' it's borne in upon me that that money won't have no blessin' upon it.'

" 'Then I'll earn some that will,' said Bob. ' I swear, one would say I was a heathen out an' out! You believe in sending missionaries out to them, but you haven't a good word for a man that's willing to do a son's duty by you if you'll let him.'

"Father only groaned and went out to the barn to pray, and Robert caught hold of me and held me. There were tears in his eyes as he looked at me.

" 'Patty,' he said, ' sometimes I've thought the time might come when you'd let go too. Are you going to?'

" 'It's too late for that,' I said. 'If you were a murderer, I'm yours for ever. I can't change.' " For a moment Patty's voice faltered, and the cold, set features quivered. A shudder passed through her, then she looked up again and went on in the dull, even tone that seemed her only refuge.

"He shivered like the ague and let go of me. Then he caught me again.

"'No, thank God, you can't change. You're faithful,' said he, and then he went out to do something Father wanted. Uncle Silas, we'd only been married ten days when those men I'd seen on the boat came up one afternoon. Robert had gone to the Point, but they said they'd wait when they found he wasn't there, and I got them supper, thinking they had something to do with the mines, perhaps. Robert came about seven, and they all sat and talked. Father's is the only house . for a good many miles, and you know we always took in people for the night; so I thought finally they meant to stay. After a while they began to talk about peddling along the lake and how many had taken it up.

"'I'm thinking of it myself,' one of them said. 'There's a young fellow near Whitehall—Tom Crandall; did you ever hear of him?—that talks of selling out, and I'm thinking of buying his outfit.'

"Robert sat by me. It was dark, almost, so nobody saw much, and he had my hand. He gripped it so I almost screamed.

"'I haven't seen him lately,' he said.

"'Not since the afternoon of June 18th,' said the biggest man, getting up, ' when you fought and killed

him and buried him under a pile of brush. Robert
Saunders, I arrest you for the murder of Thomas Crandall.'

"Robert didn't stir. The handcuffs were snapped
on him in a moment. I didn't faint or even cry out.
I said, 'Is it true, Robert?' 'Don't you answer!'
said the other man, with the warrant; 'you ain't obliged
to criminate yourself.'

" 'It is true,' said Robert, looking at me and putting
out his hands. 'It is true, and I'm a devil to have
married you; but, before God, Patty, I never meant to
murder. It was an old grudge, and Tom was half
drunk. I tried to humor him along, but he would
fight, and he said some things that made me terribly
angry. But I didn't know I had struck him hard
enough to even hurt him much, let alone killing him,
for I was bound to get off peaceably if I could, and
was just clinching with him and trying to throw him
when he fell back. I couldn't believe he wasn't going
to get up again, and when I found he wasn't I was
beside myself. There wasn't but one thing to do, and
I buried him under the brush.'

" 'I told you that money had a curse on it,' said
Father, who had just stood still, looking, 'but I didn't
know it was blood-money.'

" 'I'm not a thief,' said Robert. 'His money is with
him where he is. Not one dollar of it could I ever
have touched. Who found it out?'

" 'A man who says he'd have given one of his eyes

not to have seen what he did—Ben Searles. He was
on his way home, and saw you and Crandall walking
along, talking pretty loud. That's all he saw; but
when Crandall was missing he began to think, and he
just dropped in the store one night that he'd seen you
together. Dinsmore took it up, and went over the
ground with Crandall's pointer; but it wouldn't have
been certain then if he hadn't found right alongside
the body your own knife, with your name on the handle.
That's why we're here. It's a clear case, murder and
robbery; for Crandall had just drawn money and there
wasn't a dollar on him.'

" 'I'll never believe it,' I said. 'The killing might
be, but never the other. You shall get clear, Robert,
of that, whatever else happens.'

" 'God bless you!' he said, 'I knew you'd be faithful.' And then they took him away. They're trying
him now."

"What do you want me to do, Patty?" said Uncle
Silas, with quivering voice, after a moment's silence.

"I want you to lend me some money for another
lawyer. The State gave him this one, and he was very
kind, but I want another. I didn't tell you I had been
at Sandy Hill almost a month; over a fortnight before
the trial began. When Robert plead guilty I thought
that was the end and that there couldn't be any trial,
but it wasn't so. The lawyer said he must be defended
anyway, and he did defend him so I began to think at
last they would let him off. But when I heard the other

side they made him seem worse than anything I ever imagined. Searles's testimony and everything was pieced together so, and it seemed to prove him thief and all. I couldn't bear it. I hadn't meant to come to you, but then I thought you would help me and so I came without asking anybody about it."

"You can't change lawyers now, Patty," said Uncle Silas. "I wish you'd come for me in the beginning. You must get back right away."

"I know it; to-night if I can. It was dreadful that I couldn't get here before, but Dunning ran aground and had to wait for a boat to get him off, and so two days are lost already."

"You haven't been two days gettin' from Port Henry here!" exclaimed Uncle Silas.

"Yes," Patty answered wearily. "Dunning was kind, though, and he spoke to the captain of another boat—Fisher's boat, that starts from the Bay at seven. I want you to harness up and take me back if you will."

"I sha'n't let you go, Patty," said Aunt Huldah, rising up and trying to shake off the horrors that had come upon her. "You ain't fit. You can't."

"She's got to, Wife," said Uncle Silas, solemnly. "This ain't no time to think of *cants* and *fits*. She's his wife, and she's doin' her duty, an' we've got to help her the best way we can."

"In spite of the disgrace?" said Patty, and then throwing herself on the floor burst into wild weeping.

"Oh, shame!" she said, as after a few moments she

choked back the sobs and sat up. "Shame, to think I should waste time that way. I haven't shed a tear, and I didn't mean to; but I didn't believe you'd take it this way, Uncle Silas. Everybody that comes along says what a disgrace it is, but nobody seems to think there is anything to be done—and there's so little time! It will kill me if we can't save him."

"He's in the Lord's hands, Patty," said Aunt Huldah.

"I know it, and that's why it's so awful. 'No murderer shall inherit the kingdom of heaven.' Oh, I've said that all the way up. He mustn't die. To lose him here and lose him there too—I can't have it *so!*"

"Hush, Patty," said Uncle Silas. "The Lord's arm ain't shortened. 'Tain't for you nor me to shut Robert Saunders out of the kingdom."

"He is shut out, and we can't open the door for him," she answered mournfully. "Don't talk of it. Let us go."

"You needn't think about me, Silas," said Aunt Huldah. "Joshua Bean will look after things same as he always has, an' you stay by Patty long's you can do any good. An' when it's settled, bring her back here. She ain't fit to go back to them woods alone."

"I couldn't go anywhere else," said Patty. "If it ends well, we belong there; if it doesn't, God knows where I belong, but Father and Benoni are there anyway. There's one human being that can't throw it up to me. Benoni loves Robert, and it seemed to me a sign Robert was good as he felt to me, because Benoni shrinks away from almost everybody."

"He's one o' the Lord's own; dumb or speakin', it doesn't make a mite o' difference," said Aunt Huldah. "Now, Patty, you jest lie still a bit while I get what your uncle 'll want. 'Twon't take very long."

CHAPTER II.

ALF an hour later the shaggy Canadian pony trotted off briskly in the gray light of the coming dawn, and as the little town was left behind, shut in by the hills up which they had climbed, coming out at last on the long and nearly level stretch of land between it and the Bay, Patty drew a long breath of relief.

"They must never know there, if we can help it," she said. "Down by us, of course they do, but if Robert is cleared there'll be no need of telling here."

"But, Patty, you can't keep such a thing," began Uncle Silas.

"Why not?" said Patty, quickly. "I've come in the night. You're always coming and going on your business, and nobody'll wonder at your going now. And there are some I couldn't have know it—don't you see!—that said I held my head so high, and wouldn't look at common folks. Oh, it's low enough now! What am I made of, to think of that part of it," she added, passionately, "when, living or dying, the man I love hasn't a chance?"

18

"Patty," said Uncle Silas, turning quickly, "what awful notion you've got in your head I don't know, but if that's the best you've got to say to Robert in his trouble you'd better keep away. You can't be with him, nor no other human bein', but the Lord can an' will, and I won't hear you say he's shut off."

"But he is," repeated Patty, looking up with the same dark sorrow in her eyes. "It's no use, Uncle Silas. The first word that came to me when the men led him away was: 'No murderer can enter the kingdom of heaven.' If it had been in letters of light I couldn't have seen it plainer, and it stays by me day and night. If I say, 'God be merciful,' there it is. If I think, 'Christ died for all,' it comes again, and I know now it is our doom. I'll save him if I can, for this life is all he's got, but if he must go—oh, how shall I live! How shall I live, and know what his place is!"

"Child," Uncle Silas said, and he checked his pony at the top of the last hill. Before them lay the bay, from which the morning mist was rolling away. In the east a rosy flush was spreading; birds sung on every side, and the morning waited, cool and sweet, for the coming of the sun. "Child, just as sure as that sun will be in sight before you get to the bay, just so sure God loves you an' Robert, an' is goin' to love you whatever happens. We've got to take the consequences of our own sins an' mistakes for punishment, but he waits to be merciful, an' there ain't a creeter on

the globe he can't save, and won't, if that creeter calls
out to him. You're half dead with trouble an' don't
see, but I can't let you go on so."

" Don't you suppose I'd think differently if I could?"
said Patty, and her face settled again in the hard lines
it had worn before sudden feeling overcame her. " It's
no use, Uncle Silas. We won't talk about it. I can't
even pray for him; for it's all settled. I pray that I
may bear it, and that's all. Now we won't say any
more."

There was the old, quiet inflexibility in the tone that
Uncle Silas had learned to dread two years before,
when Patty had been with them. The intense and
narrow belief of her Scotch Covenanter ancestors had
descended to her, and even at nineteen had given her
beautiful face a sternness that made her title of "pretty
Patty Pearsons " seem utterly frivolous and out of place.
What a wealth of tenderness lay underneath the still
features and steady manner no one knew better than
Aunt Huldah, whom she had nursed through a long illness. There was passion, too, and even rash emotion
terrifying to Patty herself, who, as she fell for a time
under their sway, believed herself temporarily possessed
of the devil, and fought them down to the old level.
In matters of belief she had grown up walled within
certain formulas, the questioning of which was deadly
sin; and now, at twenty-one, the surety that whatever
she believed *must* be true gave to her the unconscious
power of any deeply rooted conviction, but at the same

time shut her in to limits so filled with justice and the inexorable qualities of God, as she defined God, that love and pity found small room for entrance, and were gradually being crowded out altogether This new, strange, absorbing love had carried her away as with a flood. To save Robert she had come to believe her mission, and had let her old sense of duty take new shape in this fierce fire in which all theories seemed to melt into the one clear fact: that the believing wife should save the unbelieving husband. Then had come the horrible knowledge of his crime and a sudden mental readjustment, this time in a permanent and inflexible mold, beyond chance of change or alteration. The idea that she could have been mistaken made all the old foundations rock under her feet. She had sinned and must suffer; and as the sad old words she had quoted came to her mind, she accepted them as her revelation and let them do their work of hardening.

Uncle Silas looked at her in silence as he drove on. Speech was useless, but his heart yearned over her: and as the sunshine streamed over the Bay and he saw the little sloop rocking lightly on the dancing blue water; his soul went out in as deep a prayer as it had ever prayed, that this sad heart at his side might know what love and pity and infinite compassion were its true portion, and might open to receive them. Patty looked gratefully into the kind old eyes as he helped her out.

"God bless you, Uncle Silas," she said. "I think things might have been different if I had had you and Aunt Huldah when I was little; but everything is settled now, past changing."

"Nothing is ever past changing in this world," he said, half to himself. "'Tain't man that has the last word: it's God."

Patty was silent, and crossed the narrow plank hastily. Uncle Silas left his pony in the accustomed place, and soon the wind was bearing them steadily on over the beautiful lake, at which she looked with unseeing eyes, counting the hours which still lay between her and the sad soul waiting her coming with a hope more often ending in despair.

CHAPTER III.

ITTING on a low bench and leaning her head against the side of the cabin, she soon yielded to the soothing, quiet plash of the water against the side of the sloop, and after the long strain slept profoundly, slipping a little so that her head rested on the coil of rope near by. Uncle Silas covered her with the shawl she had dropped and then stole back to the helm. Patty might fancy her errand unknown, but by the same curious agency which, with an always unaccountable swiftness, spreads a piece of intelligence from tribe to tribe on the Plains, or even in almost inaccessible mountain regions, every skipper on the lake knew who she was, and why she was there. Violent deeds were no surprise. All about the iron mines at Port Henry desperate and lawless men thronged, held in check only by the fearlessness of one or two among the masters; and in the Whitehall region, where the canal-boat men laid up each winter, more than one had disappeared whose fate it was impossible to discover. There were deep shafts long disused that told no tales, and to get rid of an enemy had not been a troublesome matter.

In this case all parties were well known. Tobit Saunders owned boats on the lakes and shares in the mines, and was a hard-headed, grasping man, never to be cheated by the shrewdest captain. Robert's love of adventure had made every nook of the lake familiar to him, and the same passion had made him one in various smuggling expeditions, the remembrance of which would tell against him now. Tobit Saunders, having let his son run wild for twenty years, had suddenly asserted his authority, and in the conflict which ensued ordered him never to show his face again. Public opinion was divided on the merits of the case, but all agreed that the young man had been hardly dealt with, and that Tobit Saunders simply reaped much less than he had sown.

On the other hand, no record could be more unimpeachable than that of Donald Pearsons, who, till the death of his wife, had been foreman at one of the shafts near Port Henry, and kept the men in more complete subjection than had ever been known before or since. Stern and silent, all made way for him; and the impression was strengthened by the discovery that at certain times daily he went to a retreat in the forest, a thicket of hazel bushes, and prayed with the intensity of his Scottish ancestors. A superstitious feeling grew about him, and not one of the men but regarded him as set apart from ordinary accidents and beyond ordinary passions.

As a child, Patty, who carried his dinner to him,

learned to share the same feeling, and as she grew older knelt by him and listened to the strange out-pouring of soul—couched always in the old Hebrew phrases, and being always a cry against the power of evil within.

To Donald Pearsons, Satan was a tangible form—the great adversary of souls, engaged forever in that war with God on which the old Puritans and the Covenanters as well, both seeing it from the same standpoint, looked with unchanging and unquenchable interest. Patty grew up in almost utter unconscious-ness that any other life was possible, and yielding un, questioning obedience to the command which shut her off from communication with the few young people about her. At thirteen, her mother—always silent, always sad, and after Benoni had come, the one brother, deaf and dumb from birth, a little sadder, a little more silent—had left them. The shadow lifted at the last, and the deep eyes, so like Patty's own, were bright with a light the girl had never seen. There were few words, for life-long repression was even then strong to hold them back, but she laid Benoni's hand in Patty's and said, faintly:

"Never leave him, Patty. Never."

"Never, Mother," Patty answered solemnly, and then left her as her husband knelt by the bed, his stern features working painfully as he strove for quiet and calmness. When she entered again, peace had settled once for all on the tired face, and her father still knelt, his strong frame shaken with grief he could not control. Within a week after the funeral he rented the old house and moved into what was known then, and is now, as "the wilderness," to the border of one of the first lakes in the Adirondacks.

Here the girl had grown to womanhood in a fashion full of dreariness from one point of view, but holding its own compensation as well. In spite of her creed, Patty had love for every living thing. The world was only a transitory spot—the stopping-place for a night —yet it held a beauty that filled her soul with feelings for which she had no words. Benoni's life was in the woods; and as he grew, its strange, interior life became part of him : and in following him she too learned to share it. The few hunters who from time to time ventured into the forest wondered at such a face in this still and secret place. " Beauty born of murmuring sound " had passed " into her face ;" a beauty of which she herself was not unconscious, though indifferent to it, and which moved Uncle Silas, her mother's brother —who, after years of non-intercourse, determined to look them up—in such manner that he besought his brother-in-law to let her go back with him at least for a time and have some chance for schooling.

Up to this moment it had never occurred to the father as a necessity, and he hesitated now. Worlds apart as he would have counted himself theoretically, in practice he would have made an excellent Trappist, and he dreaded any lapse from these tacitly under-

stood laws. Benoni's silence seemed to have en-
shrouded the household, and days passed in which
hardly a word was spoken. The prolonged battle
necessary to bring under cultivation the land he had
chosen absorbed the father's days, and at evening he
sat, with head bent upon his breast, lost in his own
thoughts. Patty went through her household offices
with a neatness and precision inherited and cultivated
to the highest, and then wandered with Benoni, sometimes paddling their light boat over the silent waters,
but oftener lingering in old and favorite haunts where
the deer came to drink, undisturbed by the two they
knew to be friends. To separate the brother and sister
was impossible, Benoni following her like a shadow;
and the father hesitated.

"I'll take 'em both," Uncle Silas said, heartily.
"It'll be all the same to Wife, and you haven't any
right, Pearsons, to bury Patty here. How do you suppose she's ever to get any notion o' life?"

"All she needs will come," her father answered,
gloomily. "I had rather bury her by her mother than
see her wise with such knowledge as curses the lake-
shore. But the schooling is another thing. Her
mother taught her, and I'd forgotten she needed anything more. Send her back to me as you take her,
Silas. No evil has ever come nigh her but the evil of
her own nature, and she is a good daughter."

Patty listened with dismay to the suggestion of
leaving, but her father checked all remonstrance.

"I'm not so helpless as you think, my child. I've done for myself before and I can again. You're to go back there with your uncle."

"But, Father—" Patty began.

"Child, it's settled. 'Tisn't for my pleasure you go, but because it's best and must be done. We won't talk."

This formula had long been the answer to the rare objections arising against his sometimes inexplicable action, and Patty, after the first troubled thought as to how he would do without her, felt her heart beat with a new and pleasurable sense of expectation. Uncle Silas was her mother's only brother, and in his kindly old face lay the promise of something in life she had thus far lost. He had kissed her at meeting, and she had colored hotly, so strange did any tangible demonstration of affection seem. Even Benoni she rarely fondled, and her own life had been so reticent, so devoid of all outward expression of feeling, that with a less intense nature it would have ended in the death of the feelings themselves. She followed Uncle Silas with curious looks, and he in turn looked with equal wonder at the grave and unconscious stateliness of the young girl, with her dark, quiet eyes, her crown of heavy hair, her complexion of that clear paleness which is the truest health, and her red lips closed in a firm line, belying the delicate dimples in which laughter had seldom dwelt. As she smiled at Benoni, Uncle Silas started. Life and color and youth for a moment made the still features radiant, and he wished the look might last.

"It shall, too," he said to himself. "A gal not nineteen, and as set and steady as an old woman! It's onnat'ral. I'll get some life into her face before many weeks, or I'll know the reason why."

The good man winced a little as his brother-in-law prayed, that evening, that the child who was going among a strange and godless people might not be led to worship idols with them under every green tree, and that the Lord would keep his own.

"All the goodness ain't in the wilderness," Uncle Silas said, as he rose from his knees. "There's folks in the world that believe in the Lord, as well as folks out of it."

Patty listened in silent amazement to the discussion which followed, till sent away by her father, who, as she went into the next room, said:

"You're a good man, Silas, so far as I know, but your doctrines are loose. I've got to have your word you wont try to give them to Patty. I won't have her upset and turned out of the way."

"You needn't fear. I'll do my best by them both," said Uncle Silas, and his word had been faithfully kept.

CHAPTER IV.

TO Patty, life in the little village on the border had held the excitement of a city, and this first winter in school was another revelation. Half a dozen books had made her mother's store; but Milton and the "Pilgrim's Progress" are no mean school in English, and the former she had studied till it was so much a part of her mental furniture that the lines were quoted unconsciously, and the college student who was teaching that winter looked in amazement at the girl who could not bound South America and knew no arithmetic beyond Long Division, yet spoke a language impossible to most of the tongues about her, and moved with the dignity of Eve herself. He lost his heart at once. That was the story for the whole neighborhood; but whatever private astonishment or gratification Patty may have felt she kept to herself, going on in her daily round with a calmness which soon quenched the awkward ardor of the advances made her.

"She might as well be ice an' done with it," commented one who had failed to touch her. "With that

set look, an' always goin' on just so even. You can't
make no headway with that kind o' gal."

"I don't want to make none," returned another.
"I don't want to marry a tombstone, an' for all she's
'pretty Patty Pearsons' a tombstone 's got just as
much life."

"She 's life enough if she wants to show it," said
Robert Saunders, who had come into the store and
stood now listening to the conversation. "She'll
come to it some day; but you needn't waste time,
Hiram Johnson. It won't be you that'll make her."

"Nor you," said Johnson flushing. "Tobit Saunders's black sheep ain't goin' to run off with the prize
lamb o' the flock—that won't even look at a fellow
that isn't a church member. She's handsome as an
angel—I will say that for her—but I'd as soon marry
one for all the satisfaction you'd get out of her."

Robert was silent, and soon left the group and went
toward Uncle Silas's house, where he was staying for
the night. Already her face had come to mean everything to him, and he only doubted if he could ever be
fit to win her. It was not for neighborhood talk,
however. Few knew how he planned his journeys up
and down the lake with a single eye to a night at Uncle
Silas Mann's and a chance of a talk with Patty; but
not till her year with them had ended and he followed
her into the wilderness did he feel sure what place he
had gained with her.

Patty had fought long against the feeling which had

at first seemed a temptation straight from the devil. That Robert loved her was evident in every look, but she avoided always any chance for direct avowal till he refused to be put off longer, and demanded an answer. That to her father he would be simply an unbeliever she knew, but his impetuous earnestness had done its work. Patty wept and prayed, and as a last resort, with a remnant of Scotch superstition which she christened, "seeking a leading," tried the old charm of the key and the Bible. "The believing wife shall save the unbelieving husband," was the word on which the key rested, and with the quiet deliberation of her character Patty accepted this as a guide from heaven, and decided, once for all, that she was right in listening.

This year had changed her but slightly. Uncle Silas had kept his word, and avoided any direct argument for a milder form of belief, though it was impossible to live constantly in the warmth of his sunny goodness and not become tenderer and less ascetic. And that he believed so in Robert was a strong plea for the young man. Passionate and head-strong, Robert was still of most loving and loyal nature, and in this marriage the old people believed contentment and a settled life would come. Neither interfered, though Robert begged them to speak for him, agreeing at last, however, that Patty must decide for herself and that no one could influence her against her own convictions.

The old pair, always childless, clung to her and could hardly let her go, as the last days with them came, and they looked with something of the same feeling at Benoni—whom Aunt Huldah had petted till he regarded her with a little of the devotion he gave Patty— a tall lad of fifteen, with much of her beauty but with some mental weakness which made any teaching apparently useless. The schoolmaster, who, as it chanced, had a deaf and dumb brother, and thus knew something of methods of instructing them, devoted his spare time for Patty's sake to the boy, who could, however, never advance upon the simplest reading and writing. Beyond his wood-craft, affection was his only knowledge, and he followed the very few to whom this was given with the appealing, pathetic look one sees in the eyes of a loving dog. No jealousy entered in. What pleased Patty pleased Benoni also, and when at last her answer was given, and he saw what rights Robert took, the brother's face was as content almost as Patty's own. Peace had been his portion from the beginning of his life. Patty wondered at times if it were right—if no way could be found to show him his sinfulness or give him a " sense of his lost condition "—but as she saw the expression of deep and quiet happiness with which he bared his head to the sunshine, or looked off over the lake and its circle of forest, she came to believe that in some mysterious way he was an exception to ordinary laws, and that God, it might be, spoke to his silent child in a way that he could hear and understand.

How much Benoni knew or comprehended of this

bitter and terrible grief that had now come upon her she could not tell. He had held her hand and looked at her with an intense and longing devotion as Robert had been taken from her, then turned to his father as if to promise care for him, wherever she might go.

Until the moment when Patty saw again the two old faces that meant positive, tangible help, she had felt forsaken by God and man; but now, having taken an outstretched hand, she rested at last and lay on the little bench sleeping profoundly—the first real rest in many days.

Uncle Silas went back, when sure for a little while that she would not wake, and stood near the helm. The Captain sat there smoking, and looked half curiously, half pityingly, at the man so closely connected with the tragedy. Uncle Silas shrunk back a moment. This phase of the matter had not entered his mind before, and a shadow of the family disgrace seemed to fall suddenly upon him. But, seeing that the Captain hesitated from a rude yet instinctive delicacy, he spoke first.

"Have you heard anything new about young Saunders?"

"It's gone ag'in him, an' they're goin' to sentence him to-morrow. That's the word the steamboat brought up. His lawyer tried to make it out manslaughter, an' it's my opinion he'd 'a' fetched it any other time, if it hedn't been the place was gettin' such a name. That jury didn't dare bring in a verdict for him, though they did say, 'recommended to mercy.' Judge Colden won't pay no attention to that, for you see his blood's up, there's been so much loose work. It's hard on Robert, though—hard. Now his father ain't been nigh him—won't. Be you goin' down?"

"Yes," Uncle Silas said, with a glance toward the sleeping girl. "We're on the way. Lord love him! Why did he plead guilty when he might have got off?"

"That's where you're out," returned the Captain. "He couldn't have got off, but it might have given him a little longer lease. You see it's the third murder since spring, and they're bound to hev an example. He'll be hung in ten days from the sentence."

"My God! What's that for?" said Uncle Silas aghast. "There's no law in that. They give a man a year with us."

"You're Vermont, and we ain't," said the Captain. "Its tough, but it's so. There's talk round on the lake of helping him break jail. It's an old concern, there at Sandy Hill, and there ain't a man on the lake wouldn't join; but there it is, you see. Constables flyin' round an' everything up in arms because this new judge is bound to put things through. Now there ain't a soul but what's sorry for Robert—always free-handed and no informer—and it's hard lines for a young fellow only twenty-four to go out this way, all by accident you might say. Sh-h-h! She's stirrin'. I wouldn't let her know jest yet, if I was you."

Uncle Silas walked away and sat down on a box.

The wind had freshened, and they were flying over the water with almost as much speed as the awkward little steamboat puffing and laboring before them. His eyes rested on the blue line of the Adirondacks, rising fair and sun-crowned in the distance, and his lips murmured,

" 'I will lift up mine eyes unto the hills from whence cometh my help.' Where else can it come from? Oh, poor gal! To think it's all ended this way. What can I do?"

His head fell upon his breast and he sat silent, with no power to plan for even the coming hour; only grateful that temporary oblivion had come to Patty. "If it's so that Robert killed him, as he says, by accident," he thought, "I ain't sure but what he'd better break jail. I'd have a hand in it myself to save them young things more sorrow. He might go West and start where folks didn't know him. If money's wanted, money can go that way as well as any. The thing is, with her notions, she's jest as likely to say No as Yes. I don't see, when I look at it, but what she's got to suffer right along, but I'd give a hand to save her. I can't do nothin' but pray, an' there's minutes when it seems more'n flesh and blood can stand jest to leave it with the Lord and hold still. You can do it for yourself easier'n for other folks, sometimes."

CHAPTER V.

AYS, it seemed to him, must have passed
when at last Patty stirred uneasily, then sat
up and looked about blankly till her eyes
fell upon Uncle Silas, who hurried toward her. Then
she put out her hand and for a moment held his with
a tight grasp, as if pulling herself up and out from
some slough into which she had fallen.

"I want you to ask some one here if there is any
news," she said. "They always know on the lake."

Uncle Silas grew pale and his knees shook. He had
not meant to say anything till Port Henry was reached,
and his heart failed him. Patty's eyes searched his
face with an imperative demand.

"You know something," she said. "Tell me this
minute."

"It's bad news, child," said Uncle Silas, huskily.
"They're goin' to sentence him to-morrow."

"To prison?"

"No."

Patty was silent; a dreadful silence, in which Uncle

Silas counted the knots in the fringe of her shawl, and seemed to hear the plash of each separate drop as the waves parted before the prow.

"Soon?" she said at last, in a hard, quiet voice, from which all natural tone had gone.

"Pretty soon, Patty. In less than a fortnight. Ten days, they said."

Patty threw back her head for a moment; a wild despairing movement, as of a hunted animal at bay. Then it drooped forward and she sat motionless. The day passed on. The Captain brought some coffee and Uncle Silas begged her to drink, but she shook her head. The men moved on tip-toe by her. The wind shifted, and they labored against it, tacking often, and bent for her sake upon getting to their destination speedily as might be, but Patty sat quietly through every change, her face hidden in her close bonnet. Evening had come when they lay at last alongside the Port Henry wharf, and the sun had gone down molten and glowing into a bank of crimson cloud, from which lurid lights shot over the water. Patty shuddered as she rose at last and for a moment looked off.

"Red as blood," she whispered. "I think the whole world is stained with it."

Uncle Silas looked at her anxiously, and the men followed with pitying eyes as she walked with steady step up the long street.

"Poor thing! Saunders sha'n't be left there," they muttered, and then joined a waiting group on the dock, with whom an eager but subdued discussion was held.

"We'll get over there to-night," Uncle Silas had said, and Patty had answered, "Soon as we can," falling again into silence which remained unbroken in the long ride through the forest and the reaching at last the bare and comfortless little tavern at Sandy Hill, just now filled by the lawyers who had come up to the trial. Judge Colden stood on the steps as the wagon drove up, and looked with a pity tinged with irritation at the pale and noble face which through all the trial had inclined him to a leniency he was determined not to show. Patty raised her eyes as she passed and looked at him intently. The night was hot, but the Judge shivered.

"I hoped she had gone," he said impatiently. "Her face haunts one. It hinders justice to have a criminal's relatives agonizing over him before your eyes. There ought to be a law against it. I wish the fellow had behaved himself."

"I'm not at all sure about making him the example," returned the lawyer addressed. "There are a dozen running loose who deserve it more than he."

"Exactly," said the Judge decidedly, "and they'll run less comfortably after this. The Governor may be willing to commute the sentence if she begs for it, but it's my business to see that the law is declared. I'm sorry for the girl, though."

The Judge went slowly to his room. Patty's face

stood between him and sleep, and far into the night its look of despair haunted him.

Patty begged for admission to the jail next morning but was denied; no one could see the criminal till after sentence had been pronounced. And so it came that her first look at Robert for almost a week was in the crowded court-room, with curious, pitiful eyes watching every movement. Robert's were riveted on her face, as if to draw from it the same strength which held her steady, and rested there through all the preliminary arrangements. Even when a thrill went through the people as the Judge put on the black cap and the sheriff motioned him to stand up for sentence he looked only at her, and the terrible words seemed to glance off and rebound from this strong form, worn with the alternations of hope and fear, but full still of the beauty which it seemed desecration for human hand to lay low. The judge's eyes were dim and his voice shook. Women screamed and fainted and men grew pale, but Patty stood unmoved, as if her composure must be Robert's strong rock. As silently she turned when the scene ended, and her time had come for an interview with the condemned man. She submitted quietly to be searched, and then passed into the cell where Robert sat waiting. Uncle Silas stood without; but few words were heard.

"I shall save you if I can," she said, and then holding his manacled hands bowed her head on his breast. More than the anguish of death was with them, but resolutely she put it away. Their lips met, and she rose up quiet and resolved.

"Uncle Silas will stay with you while I am gone," she said. "You know I am going to the governor for a pardon, if he will give it," and with one long look she turned away.

An hour later Judge Colden came into the hotel. "I want Saunders's wife," he said. "I have letters for her to the governor."

"You're too late, Judge," said the landlord. "She came in half an hour ago; found there was no stage until to-morrow morning and started straight off through the wood to strike the Glen's Falls road. She'll walk all the way but what she'll get there."

"Hadn't she a friend to take her over? Where's that old man? Wasn't there anybody with sense enough to see she was helped?" the judge asked furiously.

"Plenty, if she'd a-had 'em," returned the landlord. "She's got money, an' she could have gone down by canal or taken a team; but I reckon, wrought up the way she was, she liked through the woods best. There's plenty o' friends if she wanted 'em, and one she didn't, sure. Searles come in to tell her he'd take her over. There ain't a thing mortal man could do that he didn't do. Saunders don't seem to have any grudge against him, though if Searles had held his tongue I do suppose the thing would 'a' tided over. His eyes was all blood-shot, he'd cried so when he heard the sentence, and he most broke down ag'in when he looked at her; but he says: 'I've got a fast horse, Mis' Saunders, an' I wish you'd let .me take you. I'm goin' anyway on my own account, for there's some things I can say to the governor.' She jest looked at him full, a moment, an' then she says: 'To the Lord belongeth judgment, and it'll come. You are the chief one, Benjamin Searles, that led my husband into evil ways and among evil people. Your idle tongue gave him over to the law. I would die before I would take help from you or one of your name. May the Lord judge between me and thee.'

"If she'd sworn every other word you couldn't 'a' got the sense o' cussin' half so strong's you got it in that callin' on the Lord! Ben burst out cryin' an' run into the bar-room; an' we all felt kind o' crawly. She ain't the kind of enemy I hanker a'ter; but you couldn't blame her. It's tough. 'n' no mistake. Now, he didn't rob that body no more'n I did. Some miner was round, or some rovin' Kanuck, that took the chance, an' won't never let it out unless he gets too drunk to hold in. If the governor ever weakens I should say he'll weaken when he sees her."

" He will not, I'm afraid. God help her," the judge said, and turned away.

A knot of men stood near, and one of them stepped forward, suddenly, as Judge Colden passed through the door.

" Look a here, Jedge," he said, putting out one long

arm so that the way was momentarily barred. "Ain't there no way to ease matters a mite? You're comin' it rather strong, seems to me, when there's three to my certain knowledge, an' not far off neither, that deserves hangin' more 'n Saunders. Come, Jedge! Fix it so 't he can have a new trial, and we'll stand a new set o' fees and never say a word."

"We'll make it hot for you if you don't," said a rough voice, from the rear; and, at that, the trouble plainly seen on the Judge's face as he had listened to the first speaker changed to his usual expression of quiet decision.

"Make way, men," he said. "Law is law, and must be respected. I have one plain duty here, and shall do it steadfastly."

"An' stun is stun," said the first speaker, as he watched the Judge slowly ascend the stairs. "The time'll come, I'll bet my life, when you'll wish you hedn't been so durned swift and sot. Come on, boys. There may be some road out o' this, yet. I swear, I'd give my hand to stop it. I wish the p'ison old jail 'd take fire, an' I'm free to say I'm willin' enough to "——

"Hush-sh!" said a warning voice; and the men, with a backward glance, passed out toward the prison.

CHAPTER VI.

OUR days later Patty returned, and there was no need to ask how her errand had sped. Paler she could not be than when Uncle Silas had last looked upon her, but something had gone. Hope had been there, if in ever so shadowy guise; but hope had fled and only still endurance remained.

"You can go home, Uncle Silas," she said. "I do not want you to stay through it all. I can bear it now alone, and it is better you should not have it to remember."

"If I was Satan himself I couldn't leave you now, child," said Uncle Silas with streaming eyes. "Oh, Patty! I did think the governor might hearken to you!"

"He wanted to, but he couldn't," she said wearily. "He cried when he said it was impossible. Everybody tried to help me, but they said it was getting so up here people were afraid for their lives even in broad daylight. We won't talk about it. I must go to Robert."

"If he can't have a commutation he shall have a reprieve," said one of the lawyers when the result of her effort became known. "I'd be willing to take the journey for it myself."

"You are very kind," Patty answered. He had stopped her on her way to the jail, and stood now looking at her—a gray-haired man, with bluff manner but a good heart. "I do not want it. It will not help us. Robert has got to die, and why should he have a few days more of waiting in misery? He would not want it."

"He'll think you don't care, Patty," began Uncle Silas as the man turned away, but stopped before the look she turned upon him and was silent. No word of complaint came in those swift speeding days. The projected attempt to release him had been made, but the Sandy Hill authorities, warned by past experience, were vigilant. Patty herself was rigorously searched before every visit, and such strict guard was kept that little could be said.

So the last day came—a fair August morning, the mountains rising clear and calm in the distance, and the air sweet with the breath of new-cut hay. What passed in that last hour, as husband and wife sat side by side, no one ever knew. It ended, and Robert Saunders came out to his death with a steady face. The bitterness was past; and when an hour later, by special favor, his still form was given into Uncle Silas's hands, and they drove away on the road into the wilderness, Patty laid her hand on the coffin as if, man having done his worst, God had given her her own.

They laid him under the great birch near the lake, in the grave Donald Pearsons had dug when the sentence was told him. The fierce anger with which he had refused to help, or to leave the lake, had changed to a dull quiet. He aged suddenly, and Jeanette Corôt, who had been much there during Patty's year away—a reticent and energetic French Canadian—watched him carefully. Something was wrong, even beyond the cruel wound to his own pride in an unstained name or the conflict between love for Patty and the stern justice by which law he had lived.

"You've a place of your own in the graveyard; put him there," she said, but he shook his head.

"Here's where she'll want him," he answered. "Here, where they sat that day I found them and knew sorrow had begun for her. This is the place."

That night he prayed long, and Jeannette, still uneasy, heard his voice rising and falling in the intensity of supplication. Then came some curious, inarticulate sounds, and then a sudden, strange silence. Jeannette sprang from her bed and ran into his room. He had slipped to the floor and lay there, with open eyes, but speechless. The "stroke" Patty dreaded had come.

"I knew it," was all she said as Jeanette met her on the threshold the day of her return. "I knew there must be that too."

"Don't go in to him yet. You cannot bear it well," said Jeanette, pityingly, but Patty put her aside.

"Where else should I go?" she said. "I brought it upon him; but in spite of that he wants me."

The eager, searching look with which the old man had followed every sound died away as Patty came swiftly in and knelt by his bed for a moment.

"I've come back to you, Father," she said, "and I shall take care of you," and then, for the first time since her childhood, bent forward and kissed him. When she raised her head tears were in his eyes, and his lips moved in a vain attempt to speak her name.

At once the old burdens were taken up, as if no shadow shut her in with her sorrow, and she went quietly about the usual household offices.

"I can't make her out," said Uncle Silas to Jeanette a day later, as she was preparing to leave. "You mustn't go yet. She's going to break down."

"No," said the woman; "never. She will be still, that is all. Such as she go on always. I shall watch, though."

Still anxious, he could not make up his mind to leave, and, though worn and restless himself with the weary strain, for a day or two staid on. The night of the third day, hot and stifling as nights in the deep woods rarely are, he rose and went out to get a breath of fresh air, pausing a moment to look in at the invalid —who seemed not to sleep at any time, but lay with wide-open, expectant eyes—then passed out to the lake shore, the motionless and glassy water lighted faintly by the setting moon. The air weighed upon him, and he walked back and forth uneasily as, looking toward the new-made grave, he saw a dark outline near it. Could it be that the dreaded "body-snatchers" had actually found their way here? By custom the body of an executed criminal belonged to the medical students and the dissecting-room, and some who had come down to the execution resented the fact that friends were allowed to claim it. There had been whispers of an attempt at "resurrectionizing," and Searles and one or two others had, without Patty's knowledge, determined to guard the wood-road leading from the main thoroughfare to Pearsons's house. Two nights of quiet made their fear seem perhaps useless, but on the third they turned back a light wagon the occupants of which could give no satisfactory reason for their possession of various shovels and ropes, or for the fact that the horse's feet were muffled.

"Show your faces again on Pearsons's road with those things," Searles had said, "and we'll see how you like the feel of the ropes round your own necks. No blustering, now. We shouldn't kill you, but we should string you up just long enough to give you a taste of hanging and keep you from trying the same game again."

The men had driven off, swearing, and Searles drew a long breath of relief.

"I've done *one* thing for her," he said, "and I'd do more if I could. Lord! but I wish I could forget the way she looked at me!"

As Uncle Silas went forward, his hand grasping a
out stick he had picked up, the figure half rose and
e saw Patty's face.

"Patty!" he cried, dropping it. "You poor lamb,
o in. What do you mean, out here in the night?"

"Watching. That is all."

"Watching! But, child, you don't suppose that's
eeded?"

"Do you think I don't know who was in that crowd
he other day and what they wanted, Uncle Silas?
They will be on the lookout till nature has done its
work and they know it's no use. My husband's body
shall never belong to the resurrectionists. I've watched
it every night since we laid it here, and I shall watch
it till earth has her own."

"Patty, you'll kill yourself, workin' all day and
watchin' all night. Go in, and I'll stay here till light."

"No," she said, quietly. "It is my place. I shall
not die, Uncle Silas. I have got to live for father and
Benoni. We won't talk."

The old, inflexible formula! Uncle Silas turned
away in despair. Aunt Huldah he could deal with, and
had thought he knew women's ways, but he had no
answer for Patty. When the week ended he returned
home; forced to it by the girl herself, who promised to
send Benoni for them should any sudden trouble come.
As he went toward the great birch he started, for the
low mound had disappeared.

"I did it myself," she said. "It seems best. I

know where he lies but I want no one else to, so I took away all sign this morning before sunrise and put down the sods again. Uncle Silas, if we could only pray for the dead! If I could think that a long life of agony would save Robert at the last! It kills me to think where he is, and yet I know I shall not die."

"Patty," Uncle Silas answered, solemnly, grateful for this almost first word of personal feeling she had spoken to him since that morning on the lake. "Patty, child, I'd give my hand if I could make you believe what I know. Robert Saunders died a penitent man, and I believe went straight to heaven. If ever a soul took hold on the Lord his did, and he said so to you."

"I know it; but I couldn't answer, for I *knew*. I said to myself then, that if Satan deceived him it was a comfort to him and I should not speak. Even when he prayed that last hour that we might meet, I said nothing. He thought I could not. Oh, if I only did not *know!* If I only could cheat myself, and believe I should go to him, I could live and bear it. But to live and remember always that he is shut out! I don't want heaven. I would give it up for him if it were any use!"

"The Lord have mercy on you and lighten your mind," said Uncle Silas, despairingly. "Once more I say, and if they was my last words they must be the same, the Lord heard him and helped him and saved him. Patty, you slight God himself when you say he couldn't."

Patty had flung herself on the leveled grave; and, kneeling by her, once more the old man prayed that peace and light and hope might come to this burdened soul. Then he rose and walked down the wood-road, turning for the last time as a curve shut out the low house and the swaying branches of the great birch, and seeing still the motionless figure under its shadow. Tears fell as he went, but man could do no more; and, as he reached the lake and saw the mountains he had left three weeks before, the burden seemed to lighten, and his heart sprang toward the old home and the simple, loving woman who waited there and in whom faith and love were strong as in his own soul.

"We'll take Patty with us when her father's gone," he thought, "and maybe she'll come to think differently. The Lord help the poor child! I don't wonder she's beside herself, or that she's got set in a notion. 'Twon't last forever. He won't let it. I'll jest leave her in the Lord's hands."

CHAPTER VII.

EARY and heart-sick, Uncle Silas went below and, stretching himself in a bunk of the little cabin, slept for an hour or two, till roused by the heavy tread of the sailors above him. The wind had freshened, and as he went on deck he found twilight approaching, and the little sloop flying over the water.

"She ain't goin' to stay in them woods, is she?" asked the same captain with whom they had come down, and who shook his head as the sight of his passenger brought back the memory of Patty's face.

"For a spell," Uncle Silas said. "They ain't as lonesome to her as they would be to you an' me. She's happier there than anywhere: but I shall take her home with me soon as she'll come."

"That's good," the man said heartily. "I was kind o' afraid, what with the disgrace an' all, there wouldn't be nobody to look out for her, an' we was talkin' it over."

Uncle Silas flushed a little.

"All'll be done that kin be done," he said, "but the kindest thing you can do for folks sometimes is to let 'em alone. Things often straighten 'emselves if there ain't too much meddlin' with 'em, an' Patty knows where to come when she's ready."

" No offense," said the captain. " Her face sticks in my mind. I'd like to do something, but there ain't nothin' you can do."

" No, there ain't nothin'," Uncle Silas echoed, a little drearily, and went forward.

As the days passed the old routine asserted itself, and Patty, in the rare times she left her father, found herself following Benoni with a sense of rest and refreshment as the low rooms were left behind and she paddled with him on the lake, or sat by the deep trout pools while he fished. Wasted and helpless, Donald Pearsons still lived, keen intelligence in the silent face and a perfect understanding of all that went on about him. Patty never left him save when Jeanette came up for a few hours. She read to him daily; told him of all that was being done, and even consulted him as to matters of work about the clearing, gathering her answer from his looks of approval or disapproval. Patty herself had learned every secret of farm-life, and they lived in comfort from the acres which, though few in number, were brought under highest cultivation. Subsistence was certain, and something more, even if the master must live on without power of further work, and Patty's thoughts went forward to the future, if without peace, at least with certainty that they were provided for. There were times when she longed to leave it all behind, and speculated if it would be possible to move her father and seek a new home, free from these bitter remembrances. Then she put the wish aside. The old doctor from Port Henry had said decisively in one of his few visits, as she suggested a change:

"No, no. What are you thinking about? Let him go on as he is and he may live for years, but any change would kill him. You're best off here, but you ought to have some woman with you."

"Benoni is better than most women," Patty answered. "He has always helped me and always will. I want no one else."

The old doctor shook his head, and as he drove by Jeanette Corôt's hut stopped and talked with her for a few moments. Jeanette never forgot Patty's mother, who had helped her through one of the hardest spots in her own life, and had made up her mind when she left Patty precisely what course to follow.

"Have no fear," she said, decisively. "Jeanette is watching her. There is no need to trouble. All will be well when spring comes."

The short autumn days fled away and winter came, more welcome than ever before to Patty because it shut off communication with the outer world almost absolutely. Daily she shrank more and more from the thought of human faces, and retreated from any possible observation; even Benoni, who watched her wistfully, found it hard to gain her momentary attention. At rare moments she smiled—the smile so seldom seen since her dark days began. Her face lighted as if some sudden joy had come; her head bent as before some invisible presence. Then came the look of uncertainty, of perplexed and sorrowful striving to understand, changing first to despair, but soon to the cold quiet from which she was seldom moved.

" What is it?" ventured Jeanette one day as she sat by her, knitting. But the answer told little.

" It is a hope which can be nothing but a new curse. I rest in it when the devil tempts me to, but I shall be punished for every moment I dare to find comfort in it."

Jeanette looked at her sadly but held her peace. Speech was useless. Only in silence could any better knowledge come, and Jeanette prayed for such coming with an intensity that Patty could feel, but against which she hardened herself daily.

The burden of sorrow in the house left Benoni almost untouched. His serene, untroubled nature and his passion for outdoor life brought him too full measure of content to let even Patty's grief touch him deeply. Snow-shoes took him into the heart of the woods, and in them he lived a life full of purest pleasure in mere existence, every trifle that varied the story of the winter's day being noted with a loving and understanding eye.

In March, the flickering life which had so obstinately

refused to surrender went out quietly, and Patty, as
she entered her father's room one morning, found the
restless eyes closed and a look of deepest peace on the
worn face. She shed no tears.

"It is better so," was all she said. "His trouble is
over."

Benoni went to the little settlement from which they
had come, and returned with friends who remembered
him and were glad to help but who shrunk back from
the cold quiet of the daughter's manner. Patty went
with them to the little churchyard where her mother
lay, but returned the same day, refusing to spend even
a night away, and looking anxious and distressed till
the shadow of the wood once more fell upon her.

"'Tain't right," one of the old acquaintances said as
she looked after her. "'Tain't right. What I believe
is, she's losin' her mind, and some one ought to see to
her."

"You wouldn't think so if you see the clearin'," one
of the men answered. "She's a master-hand at havin'
everything jest so, an' you wouldn't say but what there
was men to do the hull on't. Things are snug as ever
I see."

"She's smart enough," Mrs. Brown answered.
"There ain't a man'll get ahead of her that way. You
ain't the only one, John Dawson, that knows how to
do; but what I say is, she'll get queerer 'n' queerer,
and go out of her head by'm'by; an' then what'll be
done? Some of us ought to see to her somehow, but

I declare for't I don't know who'd be the first to offer. The Queen o' Sheba couldn't 'a' stepped straighter; but it's awful to see how she looks jest so, an' never changes."

"Don't you worry," said Dawson. "She's young yet, and when summer comes round I wouldn't wonder if she begun to thaw out. A handsome girl like that ain't going to want for chances. Give her time to forget her troubles an' she'll take up with somebody else, an' see good days yet. There's more'n one would take her, if she'd had two husbands hung."

"They'd better try it!" said Mrs. Brown derisively. "You men are beaters, for want o' sense. I'd as soon think of makin' up to a snowdrift."

"That ain't to say it won't be done," said Dawson, decisively, and Mrs. Brown turned away astonished, but with a new light dawning. Dawson was a well-to-do young farmer, unmarried, and living with a maiden sister on his farm a few miles from the lake.

"It 'd be a good thing for her, but I will say 'tain't one mite likely to happen," said Mrs. Brown. And Mrs. Brown was right.

"There's a letter for you, Uncle Silas," the store-keeper said one evening in April, as the old man, who had aged perceptibly this winter, came into the store. "It's from down the lake somewhere, but I can't make out the mark."

Uncle Silas drew out his glasses and putting them on opened the letter slowly, studying the address and looking at the dim mark with the intentness one so often spends upon the outside of a doubtful letter instead of going at once to the final page for a solution of all questions. The hand was certainly not Patty's, and Uncle Silas wiped his glasses and began again. His face changed as he read. He folded the sheet quickly and put it in his pocket.

"No bad news, is there?" asked the storekeeper.

"No, 'tain't bad news," said Uncle Silas with a slight hesitation, and went out with more haste than usual. Aunt Huldah sat in her high-backed rocking-chair, and looked up surprised.

"I didn't suppose you'd be back for an hour," she said. Then as she caught sight of his face, " Silas ! what's the matter? Is Patty dead?"

"No," said Uncle Silas, sitting down heavily and folding his hands over his cane. "No, Huldy; she ain't dead, but she might 'a' been. Dr. Brown's written, an' Jeannette Corôt's there, seein' to things, an', Huldy—*Patty's got a baby !*"

CHAPTER VIII.

ULY had come, and nearly gone. The little steam-boat, idle through the long winter months, made her daily trips up the lake, dotted with white sails, and at times came a long line of canal boats, marshaled by an imperious little tug or moving with more than their usual slowness between great scows whose long sweeps were handled by Kanucks or old lakesmen. The steamboat had just made her landing at the Port Henry wharf; the knot of idle men and boys had dispersed, and Uncle Silas and Aunt Huldah stood there looking anxiously up the street.

"You don't suppose it's so happened she didn't get our letter?" said Aunt Huldah, her voice still trembling from the terrors of the passage. "I thought Benoni'd be right here with the wagon."

"I guess we'll walk on to the tavern, Wife," said Uncle Silas, "and I'll keep a lookout for him. They may be sick, you know."

"Benoni ain't, whatever Patty may be," said Aunt Huldah, decisively. "He's never had a sick day since he was born. I don't know as the tavern's safe, Silas,

I don't like the looks of anybody I've seen 'round here
so far, and there's no knowin' what they might do.
You ought to be careful."

Uncle Silas made no answer. A vague fear was
upon him. Twice since Dr. Brown's letter had come
they had written to Patty, but with no word of answer,
and after the spring planting was over he decided to
go directly to her, see if it might not be possible to
break up this secluded and solitary life and bring her
once more under natural influences. For no other
purpose in the world would Aunt Huldah have con
sented to leave her daily round of work and brave the
perils of such a journey, and her first sight of a steamboat, itself a comparatively new thing upon the lake,
had brought on so formidable an attack of trembling
and palpitation that Uncle Silas stood by in dismay,
and wondered if he might not better turn back at once.
The captain's wife reassured the hysterical old lady,
comforted her with much camphor and peppermint,
and devoted herself with such zeal to explaining the
machinery and philosophy of steamboats in general,
that Aunt Huldah soon rallied, and began to feel that
the price of this wondrous knowledge could well afford
to be paid in some palpitation and fluttering. But each
landing—with the attendant whistling and puffing, and
the sense that stopping was impossible, and that they
must inevitably keep right on up and over the dock
and into the woods—had been as the end of the world.
She refused to remain in the small cabin, determined

not to hide, but to face the thing boldly. She grasped the rail convulsively, and sat with fixed and fascinated eyes gazing at what each time she determined to be instant destruction.

"We've got here alive, Silas," she said, as they crossed the plank at the landing, "but I wouldn't go back that way, not for a mine. I feel as if every hair on my head had turned snow white. I want to take the stage, going back. It's the only Christian way."

"We'll see," said Uncle Silas, who thought, privately, that Patty would make it all easier when the time for return came. "What you want now, Wife, is a good cup o' tea; an' you must just sit quiet a bit while I go an' see about havin' it made."

"Tell them to have the water bilin'," Aunt Huldah said, and sank down on the horse-hair sofa in the dingy little parlor, smelling musty and damp after its months of disuse. And here, sitting bolt upright, she fell asleep with the curious suddenness at which Patty had often smiled, still grasping her bag, and napping till its fall to the floor aroused her to the sense of where she was.

In the meantime Uncle Silas had gone down to the bar-room, where the tavern-keeper was mixing a glass of toddy for the stage-driver who stood near—eyed hopefully by one or two loafing men on the lookout for a possible treat.

"I'm expectin' some one down from Pearsons's

Clearing," said Uncle Silas. "Have you seen anything of Benoni to-day?"

"Then you hain't heerd!" exclaimed the landlord, who had recognized him at once. "Well, I thought likely, but I will say it beats all."

"There ain't anything wrong, is there?" said Uncle Silas.

"Well, I don't know how you'd call it. Then you don't know anything about her movin' off?"

"I did look to see her before she got away," said Uncle Silas, aghast, but determined to have no more gossip than could be helped, and rallying all his forces. "I calkilate my letter must 'a' missed her."

"She went about the middle of June," said the landlord, disappointed that after all there was to be no new excitement. "You see, it was a fine chance. I never heerd of a better. The man that's gone in was bound to have it. She fought him a month, for he came up the first o' May, but when she found he would run up a house close by, and meant to have tavern there any how, she give in an' jest sold out. He give her a big price, though he don't tell jest how much, an' she's gone—she an' Benoni an' the baby. She didn't tell where, but folks say out West; somewhere nigh Buffalo. 'Taint easy to get out of her what she ain't a mind to tell, an' my opinion is she's most likely taken another name an' gone to farmin' with Benoni, so that baby can grow up without havin' his father thrown at him. Not that folks would throw, but she's got that notion an' it won't be driven out. Here's the very one that knows more about it than any of us, but she's close-mouthed as a tombstone. If you can make her tell, you'll do better'n most folks."

Jeanette Corôt was passing, and Uncle Silas hurried out to her. Her dark face lighted with pleasure as she saw him, then fell.

"Why are you not come before?" she said. "It is too late now. All the days I say to her, 'If you will but go to Uncle Silas!' and all the days she say, 'Never. I will never go where people always will tell my baby his father's shame, and make him suffer more than he must suffer while he lives.' Oh, it is bad you were not here."

"Come in with me. I want Wife to hear," said Uncle Silas. "She's waitin' up there, an' she'll begin to worry."

"No," said Jeanette. "You may both come with me. That is best. I will not enter that house where it is always rum, rum, rum, and Pierre and my boys drink themselves dead. Here is a wagon now. It will take you all, while I go on fast and make ready some dinner for you."

CHAPTER IX.

UNT HULDAH went wherever she was led, dumb with consternation when told that Patty was gone; eager to understand, but full of sorrow at their fruitless errand. Jeanette's hut, though only of chinked logs with floor of rough boards, was spotlessly clean and orderly, and Aunt Huldah drank the cup of tea made ready for her, with a sense of refreshment the dirty inn could never have afforded. Jeanette sat silent till the old lady had finished the light meal, and then began:

" I did think I would stay by her always, but she will go alone. Not till March will she tell me what is coming, though I know well; with my own sense, and because the doctor say I must watch. But she is so still; and when the work is done she sit and sit, and will not look up. If she would cry it would be better, but always she sit so still, and her face pale. Sometimes she smile a little, and then look so as if it were sin, and she have fear. But in March she say, 'Jeanette, you must come here a little while, and if I die you must stay always, and have care for Benoni.

I hope God will take me and the baby, and I think He will, because He will not curse me any more.' Then I say, ' That is wrong to the good God; the baby is for your blessing, and it shall be joy. You know not now how it will be when it is yours. Your heart is frozen in you now; then it will not be so; it will melt and you will be happy.' ' Never,' she said; ' that is no word I will hear. A curse is on me and mine, and I must bear it while life stays. If you love me, Jeanette, pray only that God in His mercy may end it, and I may go.'

"So I said then it was only bad to talk, and soon— in but few days more—the baby came. I tell her, ' God has given you a son, Patty, and now he will grow, and some day take care of you.' But she would hardly look, and then she cried all the day. That was better than to be as stone, and I was glad; but soon it was all passed. She nurse the baby, but she hardly will look at him; and I am angry all the time, so beautiful a babe it is. They are all the same when they begin, but soon he is no more red, but so fair and so big, and his eyes look up at her like his father, and she will start away sometimes, and then, when she thinks I see not, she look at him and she pray and hold him to her, but she will not kiss him—never.

"So one day I say : ' Patty, the baby that his mother kisses not has a curse on him, and comes to sorrow in the end. That is true, for I have seen it. Now you say, ' He is anyway cursed,' but I tell you, No. I say,

If you do as a mother with him he shall be saved that sorrow, and shall not know the evil you call to him yourself.' 'We will not talk,' she say, just as always. 'But we will,' I say. 'I shall tell you, you are wicked. He is a gift of the good God, and I myself see you put away his little hands, and he lies and looks at you, and you never a mother's word for him. It is shame. Give him to me if you will not love him. Truly I am better mother for him than you. Give him to me.' Then she cry again, and she say, 'Jeanette, if I did not love him I could bear it better; but when I see his father's eyes and know it is his father's very face and will grow more so, then I think I cannot bear it. I shall do my duty, but I shall never love him more than I can help, or if I do then I must never tell him. He is born to bear a curse, and I shall teach him that in the beginning. What he can do in this world with that knowledge I will not hinder, but he has not the life of common children and he must never think that he has. Now that is all. Never speak to me about it. I have said all I ever shall.'

"Then I went away soon. She was strong and did not need me, and Benoni, I saw well, would love it for mother and father both. For he would sit and hold it, and look as if an angel had come down out of heaven, and when it took hold of his finger with its little hand then he would smile himself with the tears in his eyes, and I had no fear but that some way the good God would see that the child had love. Then this man has come; this Slocum that will have tavern by the lake, where all the hunters will stay and the city men that come; and she tell me—when all is done, and I go to ask her what she may want of me perhaps—'Jeanette, I am going away forever. I want a new home, and everything different from this, and when everything is changed then change may come to me, too. I shall not tell anyone. I do not want to be followed or found. All I have brought my friends is sorrow, and I shall not tell Uncle Silas nor anybody. Benoni understands, and is willing to go, and together we shall make a home. Then if it ever seems good to write I shall write, but not now.'

"I said it was wicked, for you were old and cared for her, and she should say good-by; but she say, Never. That she could never do you any good, and that once gone you would forget. And so she is gone, and that is all."

"But how has she gone?" said Uncle Silas. "She wouldn't leave everything behind. Did she sell all out?"

"No, she has taken a little. Another horse that is strong, with the one you know, and a great wagon with a top; you have seen them also. This she has filled with such things as she will take, and then they travel away, and her own cow she has raised, behind; that is all."

"But where?"

"That she tells not me nor anybody."

"She's gone crazy," said Aunt Huldah, through her tears. "She ought to be looked after. She ought to 'a' come to us. Oh, why didn't we come after her, Silas? Can't we find her, don't you suppose?"

"We might, but it's no use, Huldy," Uncle Silas said brokenly. "Don't you know her yet? I'll try and get eye upon her for the child's sake, but I mistrust she'll cover her track in the end. She's been hurt to death, an' it looks to me as if she'd gone off to die alone."

"No, that will not be," said Jeanette. "One dies not of trouble. I think truly one becomes strong and ready for more. She is young, and years are in her. Some day it will be right, and the child will alter things. He has his father's name. Some day he will come to find out his own. There is Ben Searles who thinks of them, and he is gone too. Soon all I have known will be gone. He dare not go near Patty, ever, but he thinks much how he may help her. Many times he come to me and say, 'Jeanette, if ever anything is wanted she cannot get, come to me.' But she had money, and she would die before he should ever help. Ah, it is all bad together, but the good God knows."

"Then Searles has gone too? I wanted to see him," said Uncle Silas.

"Yes, he and two more—Brown and Dawson. All of that they will tell you in the tavern. They hear of rich land far by the lakes. Searles will go, because he

can never forget what Patty say to him; and he tell
me once there is a curse on the land here, and he must
go. Then Brown will go also, because they are always
together, and Dawson would not, I think, but that
Patty say she hate him for coming to her. Yes; it
was one day when the baby has but a month, and some
one tell him Slocum want her to sell and she is going.
So Dawson come, and I could hear much, because the
door is not shut. He has said he will marry her then,
and be a good father to the child, and she is very angry
and say, how dare he speak so? Then she look very
still, same as always, and she said: 'You mean well,
but never dare speak such words again. No man living ever takes Robert Saunders's place. Go!' That
is all; he talk a little, but she look as if she do not
hear and he come out, and he says: 'Jeanette, you
are close-mouthed. I ain't ashamed to have asked her.
but the Lord keep any man she fixes with them eyes.
I feel as if I'd got a stroke!' "

"Anybody might 'a' known better than to hurry that
way," said Aunt Huldah, indignantly. "If he'd been
a mind to wait a year or two it might 'a' done. I wish
it might be; for jest as long as she's a Saunders, jest
so long she'll always be thinkin' and rememberin'."

"She will never change," said Jeanette, with some
scorn. "Oh, I know well! She is old even now.
Tears will wash out such trouble when they fall from
young eyes, but she will cry—never! No, they all
stay shut in, and her eyes are hollow and soon she will

be old. Once I have seen a woman who had great
wrong done her, and she grew white-haired so none
could tell if she were old or young, and so it is with
Patty. Did I say that she is all gray this winter? Her
hair is long and beautiful; but when she is sick I comb
it out, and I see it more gray than mine, and she say,
' That is well, Jeanette. I like to seem old, even if I
must live years to be truly so.'

"Every day I pray to know what I shall do, and
how I may find to soften her heart, but if the baby will
not then I think it is not to be in this world. She
will go three day and not speak. Sometime I think
that baby must be dumb, too, because not a word will
he hear. Then I think no more and I say, the good
God knows. It is sure to be right sometime, and not
Jeanette nor anybody can hasten it. Wait."

"It's a sin to a little innocent baby," said Uncle
Silas. "It won't get the right kind o' care, I'm
afraid."

"Have no fear," said Jeanette. "She cares for it
well, only it will miss mother's love. But I think
truly it will be made up. Yes, I think it will."

"The Lord grant it," said Aunt Huldah; "but it
goes to my heart I could not have got here in time.
Maybe she'd have let me take the baby."

"Never!" said Jeanette. "She will let no one
touch it much. No; we must wait."

"You found it all straight, did you?" the tavern-
keeper said, as he the next day saw the old pair wait-

ing at the landing. The greater sorrow had set aside all lesser troubles or fears in Aunt Huldah's mind, and the swiftest way of returning to peace and her quiet routine seemed the best. "I didn't mention it yesterday, but there was a little talk in town that she wasn't quite right and maybe needed seein' after. But before anybody could settle jest what to do she was gone. I suppose it was all right?"

"Yes, all right," Uncle Silas answered, quietly; and as no after discussion in bar-room or store was able to find any new material for comment the ripple of excitement died away.

For months after their return home Uncle Silas watched the mails, and sought in every way to find some trace of the brother and sister; but as time passed on Patty came to be to them almost as one dead, and only at rare intervals they said, "Patty's boy is three"—or "five," or "I wonder if Patty's boy lived? If he did, he is quite a boy."

In her old home time did its work. Her father's generation passed away, and only now and then was any reference made to Robert Saunders's untimely fate, or a wonder expressed as to whether Patty still lived. Jeannette's lonely hut, and the home among the mountains where the old couple still hoped for news of her, alone kept full memory; and the day came when they were empty.

Aunt Huldah went first; and, with the cessation of

the constant care she had for years required, Uncle Silas's energies flagged, and those who watched his increasing feebleness said they were not to be divided long. When the end came and his will was read it was found that his not inconsiderable property had been left entirely to his beloved niece Martha Pearsons Saunders in trust for her son, Robert Saunders, to be his at the age of twenty-one, or, in default of finding these heirs, to revert at the end of twenty-one years to certain societies specified in the document.

The executors moved slowly. Advertisements at stated intervals had been provided for by the terms of the will, but these failed to bring any response. The place was kept in a certain degree of order by a neighbor, who planted the garden and divided the product of fields and orchard between his own family and the poor-house, as provided for in the will, but the old house stood empty, awaiting its rightful occupants, and though opened now and then came to have the desolate look of a deserted homestead. Vines and shrubbery grew at will, and as years went on with no word of the heirs the place came to be looked upon as shadowed by a curse—was passed hastily at night, and regarded by every child as given over to ghosts. When after long parley it was decided to rent it, lest through disuse and mold and all the silent destructive forces of nature it should fall to pieces before them,—human life being apparently the only cement which can hinder such action,—no one could be found bold enough to face the forms said to walk there or bear unmoved the mysterious sounds heard by those without as well as within.

Under the south windows grew the roses Patty had loved, creamy white and maiden's blush, and the young girls as they came by twos and threes to gather them told her story and wondered if she still lived. So the years passed, with no word or token; and the time drew near when the place would cease to burden those in charge, and pass to the hands of the new owners.

CHAPTER X.

"SEE, Henry! I really believe I am to have my wish. Isn't that a canoe pushing out from the little cove? It is, and there's an Indian in it. He is coming this way, too. Oh, how delightful!"

"Little goose!" returned the gentleman addressed, after a look through his glass. "It is not an Indian at all, but a prosaic, every-day boy, with sufficient sense of artistic requirements to wear a red flannel shirt, and thus give the one gleam of color lacking. By Jove, I wish I could catch that pose! It is superb!"

The pair, whose sketch-books were already open, went vigorously to work, and the captain came nearer and looked on approvingly.

"You won't get a better-lookin' centerpiece than him if you travel a month," he said. "I was thinkin' about him, but wasn't sure if he'd be out. Do you see that smoke curling up over the trees off there beyond the point? That's where he comes from. Lonesome enough, you'd think, for it's thirty miles from any other house; but there's a woman there your picters can't beat—face like as if it was cut out of stone, and about as still. An' the way I know anything about her is this."

Captain Rushmore seated himself comfortably. He had a fancy for this brother and sister, who found no fault, lived on deck, and were making the lakes as thoroughly their own as constant sketching could compass, while they in turn found unending entertainment in his store of lake traditions and the long experience on these inland seas.

"When I run first, it was from Buffalo to Milwaukee," he began, "and these Superior boats wasn't built. Emigrants came through all the time, goin' by way of the lakes out West, and I used to think Vermont wouldn't have an able-bodied man left in it. Bein' a Vermonter I was lookin' out for her, you see, and I used to argue it with 'em, an' tell them if they'd put as much grit into stayin' at home as they did into goin' out to fight a new country they'd have no trouble about a good livin' where they belonged. Well, one day a tall man came aboard and got tickets for Milwaukee; he had the name written on a bit o' paper. I see in a minute or two he was deaf and dumb, an' wondered at him travelin' off with an emigrant wagon. And I wondered more when his folks come aboard—a young woman, but hair gray as if she was sixty, and a baby,—and she nigh as dumb as he. First I thought they was husband and wife, but it came out pretty

soon they was brother an' sister, an' that seemed
queerer still.

"There wasn't one on board could make her talk, or
find out where she came from. Not that she was ugly,
only dead silent, with a kind of a way; and after
everybody'd tried they gave it up. She'd just sit
watchin' the shores, or else walk up and down, an'
sometimes she an' the dumb man would talk by signs;
an' that drew folks that was curious and she'd stop
short. The baby, though, took every one. I wasn't
much of a hand for babies, but that one beat all for
cuteness. The man 'd walk up and down with it. He
seemed to do the most o' the tendin', an' it was one
laugh an' chuckle from mornin' till night. There
wasn't a soul could keep their hands off it, or that
didn't wonder about the mother. I don't say she didn't
look out for it, for she did; but never a word to it,
when you'd think it was more than flesh an' blood
could do not to talk back to the little thing that was
just runnin' over with pure happiness.

"Well, there come up a heavy storm, as there does
sometimes in July when you're least lookin' for it, and
a tremendous wind—about the heaviest wind I've ever
seen for that season—and we lay by for a day before it
seemed best to go on. The men went ashore, gunning
around, and this deaf and dumb Pearsons among the
rest. He didn't come back till just dusk and then he
went straight to the sister, and they were talkin', their
fashion, a good while. Then she came and asked me

when I should start on. I said about midnight, I reckoned, for the wind seemed easing up, and she said then they'd put the team an' the cow ashore, for they'd made up their minds to stop there. 'You're full twelve hours from Milwaukee,' says I, ' an' 'tain't anywhere's near anywhere. There ain't a village within fifty miles.' It would do just as well, she said. She was used to wood-life, and her brother had found a place he liked. Well, I was too taken aback and too skeered of her to say much one way or another. I give her back the difference in the passage-money, and I looked on sort o' dazed while they got ready to go off. The Company had a store-house about thirty miles down that tapped the back country, and one man lived there in charge— a man that hunted and trapped, winters, when the lakes was closed—and for all it wasn't any of my business, I made up my mind to see he had some eye on 'em, for I felt as if I ought to stop their gettin' off there.

"However, they went, and I sha'n't forget the night. These big sand hills ain't the cheerfulest company that ever was, when the moon's shinin' an' the water looks black as ink against that white line o' sand. She stood with the baby when she was all ready, an' he put out his arms to me. I took him a minute, an' he looked at me with his big dark eyes, solemn, as if he knew it wasn't just right, and held one o' my fingers that tight I couldn't but just make him let go. Seems sometimes as if it never has. I've dreamed time an' time ag'in of

that little grip, an' the kind o' hold it's kept on me.
The last look I had of 'em was that big prairie schooner
an' its white top going off into the woods—the cow
moo-in' behind just as if she didn't mean to be reconciled—and them big heaps o' sand, like big graves as
much as anything. The wind lifted an' I had to go on;
but I didn't get over it in a month, they stuck to me
so, an' I never could feel easy when I remembered
'em.

"Well, Cranstoun kept an eye on 'em, just as I knew
he would when I told him. They'd picked a pretty place,
with a good bit of land that wasn't all sand-blown.
You see that inlet makes up into shore. Well, the
other side the point a little stream empties into the
lake, and half a mile above it broadens out into quite a
sheet o' water, a good mile across and full o' fish. All
'round that is sugar-bush, where the Indians used
to come to make sugar, and there's plenty o' birch
and hard-wood. 'Tain't a bad place, if one had a neighbor or two. I did think I'd manage to stop there
some day, but it was a good three year before I saw
one of them. Cranstoun told me about 'em always.
They'd built a good log-house. He'd turned to and
helped 'em, an' she worked full as hard as the men, and
seemed to like it. Cranstoun stored such things as she
ordered and had brought up from Chicago till they got
ready to come for them, and Pearsons had a big pack
of furs every spring—bigger'n Cranstoun's—an' took
in considerable money that way. They got their land

into good shape and raised a good deal, so't they were well enough off.

"The fourth year, the first trip I made, Pearsons come out himself in a canoe, lookin' just the same, an' there was that baby, a little fellow, handlin' his own paddle like it had been born with him. An' so they've done every season since; an' I never see that boy but what I want to carry him off. His laughin' ended when he was a baby; he's about as silent now as the rest; but you'd say he was a young prince. I've seen that same look in some of the Indians : not a rag but a blanket, but walking as stately an' easy as if they owned the globe. Cranstoun's a regular slouch, but you just look at that boy."

The canoe was near, the boy paddling with strong, swift strokes, apparently unconscious of the admiring looks from the knot of passengers who had gathered near. To the general disappointment, there was merely an exchange of packages, the boy tossing one lightly to the deck and receiving one in return from the steward who had stood waiting.

"Come aboard, why don't you?" the Captain called, but was answered by only a smile, as the canoe turned and retraced its way.

"That is an outrage," said the young lady, "when I meant to hear him speak and to sketch him. He has a curious unconsciousness, Henry, that I never saw in an American boy of that age. He looks like one of those lithe, picturesque Neapolitans, but his eyes have

no indolence in them. They mean action, and a soul,
if eyes ever did. Why did he go?"

"Don't idealize him," said the brother. "His occupation made him picturesque in spite of himself. I
admit he has rather an unusual head and face, but he
is much better at a distance than near enough to hear
his twang and see his manners."

"Cynical as usual," returned the sister; "but, all the
same, I wish that we were going to stop here and I
might see these people. Do they allow anybody to go
near them?"

"If anybody wants to go, how're they going to
hinder it?" said the Captain, his eyes still following
the canoe. "It beats me how I want to get hold of
that boy. I've been there. I went up there three
years ago with Cranstoun, an' she remembered me, an
said so. The place was neat as wax; you never see
anything more so; and about as nice a little farm as
you'd ever want to look at. Grapes and apples,
plenty of 'em—for all they say you can't raise 'em along
here because the lake winds take 'em, and everything
freezes up solid a good six months. I went to see if
she wouldn't let me take that boy home with me and
give him some schooling that winter. 'I thank you!'
she says, stiff as a queen. 'What he needs to know I
teach him myself.' 'Well,' I said, 'I don't say but
what that's very good, far as it goes, but a boy like
that wants something more than the three R's. I'll
get him a chance with the Company if you say so. I

can do it easy, for my three is gals, an' I've no boy of
my own to work in. He'll make a good sailor. You
think twice before you say, No.' The boy was there
listening an' his eyes shining. I knew he'd be willing.
'Go out, Robert,' she said. He looked as disappointed—
for you see we'd got pretty good friends, by an accident I hain't told you about—but he went straight
along. Then she said, standin' up so't I couldn't do
less than take the hint, 'I thank you, but he needs
nothing more than he has here. I cannot have his
mind disturbed. If it is, and I find it going on, then I
must go farther, where man cannot intrude. His home
is with me; never with man.'

"I 'spose it sounds queer, but I sort o' sneaked away
as if I'd been tryin' to do her a mortal injury, and somehow or other I hain't had the courage to do it again.
She's a way I never saw; still and steady as a rock. She
don't change, except that somehow her face is catchin'
up with her hair a little more. The boy don't look
put upon, but it's my opinion he'll break loose some
day, and I'm waiting for that. When he does, I'm
ready for him; the sooner the better."

"I shall want to know when the time comes," said
Miss Anstiss, as the Captain rose, and stopping a
moment to look at her brother's sketch turned away,
nodding approval.

"You can do better," she said; "try once more—he
is still in sight."

CHAPTER XI.

ROBERT in the meantime had reached the inlet, and vanished behind a group of trees —a white birch standing, as nature delights in placing them, against a back-ground of dark pines on which every delicate spray and twig stood out in full relief. Here the boy sprang out as the canoe grounded, drew it safely up in the white sand and turned to the thicket of alders. A step or two farther and they parted before him, showing a flat rock over which the slender branches had been woven together, forming a natural roof, while a wild grape-vine, heavy with unripened clusters, ran at will over the broad support.

Moss and leaves thickly massed in one corner showed the spot to be a frequented one, and sitting down there Robert opened the package eagerly, pausing a moment as a whistle from the lake showed that the propeller was rounding a point. Sheltered against all observation from the mainland, the spot was open to the lake, and Robert looked off over the blue water gleaming under the July sun as if storm and wind

could never come. At the west lay the long sand-
dunes, white and hot, shifting always before the lake
winds which from day to day shaped them into ever
new forms. Far to the north the blue line of the
Mackinaw bluffs lay clear against the sky; the trans-
parent northern air seeming to bring them nearer
and give every outline with sharpest precision. Nearer,
a heavily-laden little sloop tacked, and sought to make
headway against the calm, and on the shore at his
feet the waves lapped softly. Robert's eyes roved
over all, a dreamy light softening their clear darkness,
then turned again to the books which had come from
the careful wrappings. Three or four battered volumes—Plutarch's Lives and a history of Greece—worn
with use and time, and a leaf missing here and there,
but looked at with delight by the boy, who, lying at
full length upon his rough couch, read steadily till a
horn sounded. Springing up, he pulled away some moss
growing apparently in the rock and disclosed a natural
shelf holding several volumes. The new additions
were laid in with loving reverence—one would have
said who watched the boy's face—the moss carefully
replaced, and then he darted off through the trees with
the speed of a young deer.

Patty Saunders had kept her word, and as her baby
grew from toddling, clinging, loving helplessness,
fondling her even when most sternly put away, into a
child who would not learn silence yet came to know
that silence must be his life, she watched the change

with the only satisfaction her sealed heart could know. Joy had no right in her life or his. Both were under the wrath of God and must walk softly before the Lord to avert even ever so little, the retribution hanging over him. As the child's laugh rang out at times in response to some quaint gesture of Benoni's she frowned and silenced him till he shrunk away, learning at last that before her no natural impulse must be followed. Born under such conditions as he was, his joyousness seemed always to his mother an outrage; an unaccountable perversity of nature, to be rooted out if possible. So, as the child grew to understand, he lived two lives: one of silent and constant repression; the other as silent, in one way, but abounding with a satisfaction which was his salvation. To the great deerhound Robert repeated all he knew and all he thought, and Cæsar answered dog-fashion, with loving eyes that seemed to understand and wait for each word.

"God is angry with the wicked every day," were the first Bible words taught him by his mother, long before any meaning could enter into them, and as his baby lips repeated the hard saying, Patty's look of satisfaction, that the time of positive training had at last begun, staid with him. That God made everything had already been learned, and as months went on and he questioned more and more, he asked one day:

"What made God make the wicked, if he is so angry with them? Are you wicked?"

"Yes, Child," Patty answered, after a moment's

strange look. " We are both very wicked. We deserve
to go to hell and burn forever; and we shall, if we do
not repent."

"To burn forever!" the child repeated. "Is that
what God does to people?"

" Yes."

" Then God is wickeder than everybody. I hate God,
and I won't think about Him."

There was a horrified pause. Then Patty said:
"You are wickeder than I thought, Robert. You
must love God."

" I hate him," the child repeated decisively.

Patty stood looking at him. So the curse was beginning to work already, and her battle with positive
evil had begun. To her troubled mind the defiance in
the child's dark eyes seemed the outlook of an actual
demon, to be cast out at any cost to herself or him.

" Kneel down and ask God to forgive you for saying
such things," she said. " You are a very wicked boy.
How dare you!"

" No, no," Robert said, and as she urged, and at last
threatened punishment, the " No, no," came with even
more decision. Up to this point in their lives there
had never been collision. Her few commands had been
obeyed at once, but the two wills met now in a battle
neither could ever forget. Three days the struggle
went on; Patty determined to conquer and force some
expression of sorrow, and Robert setting all his baby
strength against it. But when the fourth came, and

Benoni, who had till then waited passively, saw the child still resolutely refusing, but with pale little face and eyes from which life seemed slipping away, he came forward passionately and took him into his arms. Neither whipping nor starvation had brought anything but the one answer. Patty had prayed over him for hours, while the exhausted child slept; then wakened him to fresh questioning and fresh punishment, till at last, as Benoni came between them and stood with flashing eyes and his father's look on his usually gentle face, she turned from both and went to an inner room. She had done her duty and evil was strongest. What remained but to confess herself beaten and to let the predestined fate work itself out? Her own child defied her, and even her brother had turned against her. Dominated by one idea, Patty's brain had ceased to work in any normal way. Evil hedged her in, and she came to believe herself accursed for disobedience, if not heir to some unknown curse of a former generation under whose blight she as well as her child, weighted already by his own inheritance, must struggle. Nothing remained now for this wholly perverted nature, she thought, but to guard it even more carefully from human contact, and, if he must live, let it be apart from all temptations save those of his own temperament.

She looked for constant defiance, but to her surprise it did not come. The whole conflict seemed to have passed from his mind. He clung to Benoni, it is true, but with no apparent resentment toward his mother, who on her side, as months rolled into years, prayed with ever increasing earnestness that God's will might be to remove this child of sin and sorrow before he had committed any terrible outrage against man's law that should condemn him to some lower depth of that endless torment, the position of all save the predestined few. At times she tried to make him understand that God could love as well as be angry, and had sent his own Son to redeem people, but to the boy in whose mind was an unfading impression of her first teaching this seemed simply another outrage from the strange Being whose only joy was in destruction.

To Patty this was the final and most convincing proof of the innate malignity, the hopeless wickedness, of his heart. Day after day, in anguish, she prayed for some power that might soften the stubborn nature and show it the truth; but as time passed she came to believe this seeking to alter immutable decrees as only one more sin. Life merged more and more into fixed and silent routine. That Benoni and the child should be comfortably clothed and fed, that the farm must be well kept up to insure this end, was her sole worldly thought. Beyond this her mind ceased to question life or death, and one day was as another.

So the boy's life went on, finding all childish joy or growth outside of anything she had to give, and clinging to the dumb uncle as the only tangible human love. At times, moved by the passionate, loving nature, his inheritance from both parents, he flung his arms about her. Patty never repulsed him, but she made no response, and these outbursts now seldom came.

Cranstoun was the only link with the outer world, and, though practically a hermit, to Robert he represented all the wonderful knowledge and life that lay beyond these lakes and forests. Speech itself might have been almost forgotten but for Cæsar, to whom he talked all day, and Cranstoun, who in their occasional meetings told all he knew to this strange child, who came close to him, searching his face with eyes that seemed always asking for something they had never seen, and whose rare smile was as sweet and radiant as that his mother's face had sometimes worn in her girlhood. Cut off from all common life, he learned that of the woods as Benoni had done before him, and while he gained from him every art of the hunter or fisherman, it was Cranstoun who gave names and definitions, and supplemented the practical lessons by all the wood lore he had gained in his long life as lumberman and trapper. No Indian boy ever knew better the resources Nature held in trust for him, and already bow and arrow and rifle were familiar weapons. So he "grew in sun and shower," happy in the free life, yet with this look of always unanswered questioning.

Once having learned to read, he studied the few books brought with them till he knew them almost word for word. In the winter evenings Patty had him read to her from the half dozen old classics on the shelf, and Robert pored over the "Book of Martyrs," and knew all the story of "Paradise Lost," before he was nine years old; gaining a command of stately and unexpected words amazing to Cranstoun, who had no such vocabulary.

How to help him to something more was often in his thought. His own life was solitary as the boy's, and offered no solution of the problem; but time moving on brought, as time will, new combinations—the key to all lying in the child's unconscious hand.

CHAPTER XII.

ROBERT'S first lessons in managing the little canoe, made for him by an old squaw who brought berries, had been on the small sheet of water from which the creek flowed to the great lake; but as he grew older and more adventurous the narrow space ceased to satisfy. Beyond the inlet, lay access to passing vessels, and in Patty's mind there was long a dread that these men, rough and lawless, she supposed, like the Champlain sailors, might in some way attract and influence him. Now and then some one hailed him or threw out a rope, a tacit invitation to come aboard, but the boy shrank more and more from any advances, and Patty ceased to feel anxiety.

Once or twice, when the supplies to be brought up were light, Benoni and he had gone down to the store-house by canoe; a trip looked forward to with the delight other children find in Christmas. This season, the wood-road being still well-nigh impassable from late rains, the same mode was to be adopted. Heretofore they had reached there just after the departure of the propeller, seen thus far by Robert only at a distance, and still an object of mystery and even distrust; but on this occasion the "Oswego" was a day late, and when they reached the storehouse had not yet come in. Cranstoun welcomed them with the heartiness he always had for the two, and Robert shared his bunk that night. Just before dawn the whistle sounded. Cranstoun rose hastily and went out to the dock to receive the few packages for the settlement fifteen miles back and deliver those intrusted to him for the Company. Robert lay quiet, watching the lights and wondering what the great boat was like, then sprang up to see for himself. Cranstoun was busily occupied, and Robert looked with fascinated curiosity at the white column of steam pouring up, and the colored lights on the flag-staff; then crossed the plank and stood on the lower deck.

"Here, youngster; take this below," some one said, putting a basket in his hand, and Robert, who had already looked down a ladder and into a mysterious cave he burned to penetrate, seized the basket and slid down. Once there and in full view of the red light from the boiler-fires, all thought of time and place fled, and he looked with a half fearful fascination at the roaring fires, the black bulk of the machinery, the hundred strange adjuncts of this force of which he knew absolutely nothing. Even when the framework trembled as the screw began its motion he still stood absorbed till the whistle sounded, and then sprang up the ladder. Already the dock was far behind.

"Let me off! Let me off!" he cried, but in the bustle no one heard. For a moment he thought of jumping overboard and swimming back; then a new thought came. These boats stopped at stated times at the store-house. In a week at most the "Oswego" would return, and what might not be seen in a week? Robert sat down on a box and reasoned out the matter with quiet deliberation. That he had no money and might be put off at the next landing did not occur to him, nor that all would be frightened when they missed him. Accustomed to be gone a week or more in the woods with Benoni, this demanded no more anxiety than that. Cranstoun would know he was soon coming back, and would tell Benoni; and he had thus nothing to do but accept it all as a rare and wonderful outlook into the wide world he longed to see. Somebody would speak to him by and by, and he could explain it, and in the meantime he would look at everything, and see how people lived in these floating houses. So, having investigated as far as the dim light allowed, and decided that sunrise would help him and he would wait for that, he went up the stairs to the main saloon, and, sitting down on a sofa, soon fell asleep. There the steward found him when he came to make ready the breakfast tables : an unexpected and picturesque little figure in his buckskin leggins and moccasins and his red shirt, and most evidently not a legitimate passenger. Roused at once and ordered to give an account of himself, the indignant steward swore with such energy as to bring out the Captain, who as he heard the boy's name looked curiously at him.

"It's a queer chance," he muttered. "The very same boy. Hold your tongue, steward. I'll see to him. You come with me. Give an account of yourself," he added as he pushed the boy into his own room and threw himself into a chair. Robert's grave eyes met him steadily. The abrupt manner did not daunt him, and as he told why he was glad to have been carried off, the Captain rubbed his hands and laughed.

"It's all right," he said. " Keep still awhile, till I've had forty winks, and then we'll talk."

Robert sat quietly as the Captain threw himself on the narrow bed, looking about this wonderful room hung with maps and charts and mysterious instruments, with two shelves filled with books—at which he looked with deepest astonishment, never having supposed the world held so many. Before the survey was half completed the steward knocked, and the captain, awaking with a promptness only equaled by that with which he had slept, led the boy out and gave him a place at his own table.

"It's the child of some folks I took through when he was a baby," he said, "and he's come to make me a visit. He'll go up to Superior with us."

Robert smiled with the look which had already won

the Captain, whose only boy had died the previous year, and before the day ended felt that his wildest dreams were more than realized. Silent as life had made him, he found words for all these people, who looked at him with friendly eyes and questioned him about his life with an astonishment he could not understand. He was no boor, for even in solitude Patty had preserved all household decencies and trained him to a decorousness and neatness which were part of her own nature; and, with no other child on board, he became temporarily the center of curiosity and attention. So strangely ignorant yet so wise, with an unconsciousness which nothing altered, and a beauty of form and face setting him apart from common children, he went his own way through that week and found it crowded with more experience than his eleven years had ever known.

That first morning, he had looked up to find a pair of keen gray eyes fixed upon him, and had answered the look with such quiet scrutiny that the owner, a young engineer on his way to a post at one of the copper mines, decided that here was a character to be studied, and at once made advances, talking with him as no one had ever talked before and growing more interested every hour. Fresh from an Eastern college among the mountains, Dwight Lockwood drank in the sights and sounds of this strange, new land with wonder and delight, and Robert gave him more of its heart than he could have gained in a year of living it.

The propeller lay for a day at the little mining village, the end of the route, while the men wheeled the bars of ore on board, and Robert with his new friend went down into one of the mines with the manager, an old acquaintance of Lockwood's: a man with a worn and almost haggard face, who paid little attention to the boy, till, as they were ascending the shaft, the light fell upon his upturned face.

"What's the matter, Searles?" said Lockwood, startled. "You are pale as a ghost."

Searles laughed uneasily.

"It's the light, Dwight. You look greenish, too. Where did this boy come from?"

"Robert? Oh, he's a friend of the Captain's, prospecting with me to-day."

"Robert! Robert what?"

"Robert Pearsons Saunders," the boy said quickly. He did not like the man's tone. Searles was silent till they reached solid ground again. Then he asked:

"Where do you live?"

Robert answered—as he had done to all—

"Down the lake."

"With your father and mother?"

"With my mother and Uncle Benoni."

A child came running to meet them; a little girl, with long fair hair and quiet gray eyes. She looked shyly at the boy. Searles had taken his hand and was looking at him with an expression Lockwood could not understand. Robert in turn gazed steadily at this most astonishing apparition—the first child he had ever seen, save the year before when a boy on a passing sloop had called to him in his canoe. He stood silent but considerate, as she ran to her father and took his hand. Then Searles bent to her.

"Ruth," he said, "this is some one I have wanted to see; an old friend. Kiss him."

The words might have applied to Lockwood, who put out his hand, but Ruth, whose eyes were fastened on the boy, suddenly came close to him, then put her arms about his neck and kissed him; so strange and unexpected an act to Robert, who never since his babyhood had felt the touch of any lips, that he colored deeply. Then his eyes filled with tears repressed in a moment, but he took Ruth's little hand, and so the two walked to the landing, Searles now and then looking back at them. At night the boat started on her return trip, but not before Lockwood had arranged to keep up some communication with Robert, who at the end of his week's journey reached the store-house once more, with the sense that all the world lay behind him.

Cranstoun, at first deeply troubled, and inclined to believe the boy had run away, decided otherwise at last, and so reassured Benoni, who, though Robert swam like a duck, was convinced he had fallen from the dock and been drowned, and required the most vehement shakes of the head, and the most emphatic noes, written with a bit of charcoal on a shingle and held before him whenever his ominous signs indicated that the fear had come up again. Made easy after much effort, he returned alone, Cranstoun promising to bring up Robert himself when the propeller return-ed, and Patty, after the first shock of knowing him gone, accepted it with a curious apathy. Her firmest intention for him had been overthrown, but predesti-nation settled any questioning and made her submis-sive to a result she had no power to alter.

Thus Robert on his return met no reproaches, and in the excitement still strong in him even talked with freedom of what he had seen and done, and ques-tioned eagerly to discover if she had any knowledge of this wonderful outside world.

And another question had arisen. Who was his father, and why had he never heard of him? Everyone had asked, "Is your father dead?" and exchanged significant looks as he answered, "I don't know," and now he determined to find out. Till this journey it had never occurred to him to wonder if there were anyone besides this silent pair on whom he had claim, or who meant anything in his life, and, indeed, but for Cranstoun he would have been in absolute ignorance of the existence even of outside ties. And he dreaded now to ask. The wall of silence between mother and child had grown with each year till it seemed impene-trable, and for days, as his thought questioned, his lips refused to frame the words, silenced as if an unseen hand had been laid upon them.

The three sat one evening about the crackling fire, Robert with the Bible, from which he had just read aloud a chapter in Lamentations, still open upon his knee. Patty's eyes were fixed on the shower of sparks flying up the broad chimney, and Robert, who had been watching her face, spoke suddenly:

"Mother, I want to know who my father was."

Patty turned slowly and looked at the boy, who met the look firmly and quietly.

"Who told you to ask?" she said.

"Nobody, but I want to know."

"He is dead," she said, after a long pause. "He died before you were born."

"Here?"

"No."

"Where?"

"We won't talk," Patty said, over whose face had passed a shadow. The time had not come for the full story. Not unless some sharp need of warning arose would she re-open the old wound. The boy was here, unhurt apparently by his glimpse of the life from which he was outlawed. Wait till he showed some sign of harmsome intention of again seeking it. Then she must speak, and show how God's hand shut him in, but not till then.

"Tell me, Mother," he urged, more and more curious as he watched her changing face, but she made no answer and soon left him.

Benoni patted his head softly, and Robert still sitting

before the fire—only a pine-knot lighted for the reading —wondered, and from the scanty answers began to construct a positive conception of what this father might have been, and to plan some new method of drawing more knowledge from his mother. But any planning then or in the months that followed proved futile. Patty was silent, and Robert took refuge more and more in the life opened up to him by the package of books sent by Lockwood; for, cramped as to means, but unable to forget the boy whose eager intelligence had appealed to all his sense of helpfulness, the young man had sent down to a friend in Chicago and asked him to buy, at a second-hand-book stall known to both, certain school-books adapted to a boy of twelve, and told Robert to be on the lookout for a package when the "Oswego" went up again.

And so it had chanced that, a month after his return, the boy had come into possession of a "lot" taken from the stall and sent precisely as it had lain there; soiled and grimy with dust, and, to a child accustomed to the profusion and beauty of school-books in our modern system, valueless, and even ridiculous. To Robert it was a mine of wealth. He received the package as Captain Rushmore tossed it down to the canoe with a good-natured, "Come again before we stop running," as if it had been a gift from heaven, and rowing to shore sat down in his nook to examine it, too eager to wait till at the house. A copy of the old Malte-Brun geography; a history of the United States; an arithmetic, and a tattered copy of the "Child's Book of Nature;" half a dozen pamphlets; two or three sermons; the report of some charitable society, and a thicker one—a paper-covered copy of "Ivanhoe." Something in this attracted him, as he turned over the leaves. Here was conversation, but very different from "Pilgrim's Progress," the dialogues in which he knew by heart. He turned to the first page, and in spite of much he could not understand was soon lost in the story. Noon passed but he did not stir, and when late in the afternoon Patty came in search of him he lay in the white sand propped on his elbows, the book open before him, turning the pages with an absorption from which he did not arouse till called imperatively. Then he sprang up and looked with bewilderment as he saw the sun low in the west.

Patty looked at the books—she had known they were to come—took them into her hands for a moment with a sudden movement that was almost a caress, then laid them down. All this life was behind her. Was it well that the child should even begin to know it? She looked at them and then at him. For a moment he thought she might toss them into the lake, but if such a thought came it was dismissed. God would lead the lad as Ishmael was led, and if to destruction no word of hers could stay it. She must wait as she had waited since the catastrophe of her youth. Robert gathered up the books, and as he did so a letter fell from one of them, written in large round hand that he might read it more

easily, but, even so, a hard study to the boy who knew
no writing save his own straggling copies of his
mother's texts. Lockwood wrote:

"I send you these, because they are what you need first and
most. I want you to try and write every week what you have
learned in the history, and while the boat runs send it up to
me, as we planned. I shall send it back corrected, and in that
way you will learn so that by-and-by you will write easily. I
shall help you all I can and never forget you. God bless you
my boy.

"Your sincere friend,   DWIGHT LOCKWOOD."

Robert looked with a new feeling of envy at the
easy, flowing hand, in such contrast to his own cramped, uneasy letters, but then, with the sense of something friendly and strong beyond the narrow life in
which he was bound. Over the "God bless you" he
frowned, then sat with his eyes bent upon it, as if
some hidden meaning would discover itself. In this
Bible which he read daily to his mother, God still held
the place she had made plain to him in his babyhood:
avenger, stern judge, destroying all who opposed him,
and even allowing the murder of his own Son. Such
a God might be feared: there might even be a sense of
wonderful power—the power that came in the crashing thunder and fierce lightning of this far north; but
that any one could write "God bless you," as if such
blessing were a possibility, was a state of things of
which he had no comprehension. Was not the whole
story of "Paradise Lost"—the never-ending fight with
Satan first and then with man—and even the wild bat-

tles of the Revelation, proof that only war and suffering pleased this awful Power? The Gospels ended always in the death of One for whom the boy sorrowed as for a near friend, and the beauty of whose teachings had made its own place in his heart, but all was shadowed by the thought that even he had been forsaken in that last moment of agony. With a yearning born of his lonely life, and a thought far beyond his years, he longed to understand; but at last, as older minds have done, dismissed it all as incomprehensible, and read his appointed portion mechanically, ceasing to question.

CHAPTER XIII.

CONSTANT repression had not killed Robert's natural joyousness, but had subdued it to a sustained inward cheerfulness seldom the portion of boyhood. As the months passed, Patty supposed he had forgotten the brief week of revelation, and went her silent way with small thought that those days in which human voices had been in his ears, and the sense of something beyond the starved life of home, had filled him with eager longing for more and more. Ruth's face and the touch of her fresh little lips came to him, or the strong clasp of Lockwood's hand; and, working in the field or drifting down the creek in his canoe, he reached out hungrily for the new life, yet shrunk from telling his thought or seeking to escape. Before the lakes closed another little package had come to him: this time a history of the world; a thick volume, the dry skeleton of which Robert filled out in the long winter evenings as he lay on the bearskin before the fire, longing for some one who could answer the thousand questions filling his mind. His vivid imagination—until "Ivanhoe" had aroused it, an

105

unknown quantity—gave life and color to the dryest detail. With a memory fresh and unburdened by any load of early rubbish, he seized these books and made them so his own that years afterward a word would recall whole pages. For three years this had gone on, his shelf of books gradually filling; a Latin grammar and reader having been the latest additions. He ceased to be Robert Saunders, and, as he set his snares or sped on snow-shoes through the wood or over the lake, became Ivanhoe, or John Smith, or Hercules; whatever hero was just then uppermost. Wearying for the sound of voices, he kept up his old fashion of talking with Cæsar, and made the woods ring with imaginary conversations, personating a dozen heroes at once.

Patty watched him with growing uneasiness. In the old life, silent as her own, she had felt security; but this eager interest, this impetuous, absorbed intensity, held all possible dangers. More and more like his father, the boy suddenly growing into height and almost manhood, his fourteen years seeming far more like twenty-one, she questioned with sharpest anxiety what means might check the onward progress. This steady happiness was sheer defiance of God's will for him. Perhaps the time had come to tell him all; and again she prayed and struggled, and at last came to a resolution holding, to her mind, the best solution of all perplexities.

Robert came home one evening bearing a string of pickerel caught through the ice. April had come, but

they were still shut in; though now he had begun to
count the weeks before the " Oswego's " trips would
begin, and to turn over his books and papers with an
eager desire to once more open communication with
his friend. He had settled, too, in his own mind that
the time had come for change; exactly in what way,
he had not determined, but he must see Lockwood and
talk over the future. He would write to him to-night
some of the thoughts that had been going through his
mind as he fished.

Patty took the fish from him as he entered, and
began preparing one for his supper; and Robert, after
he had made ready for it with the neatness which had
become second nature, went toward the shelf where
the books and his writing materials had always stood
—to find it empty.

" Where are my books, mother?" he said, thinking
some new arrangement might have been planned, yet
wondering at any change. Patty turned slowly. If
she changed countenance at all it was not perceptible
as she pointed to the fireplace.

" What!" Robert said, unable to take in her meaning.

" They are burned," she said, calmly.

Robert stood for one instant utterly dazed at such a
catastrophe, then sprang forward and caught his
mother's arm. Patty met his look with firm but di-
lated eyes.

" How dared you? How dared you?" he gasped. His

face was pale with passion. Curious little dents came and went about his nostrils.

"My God!" Patty said low, and as if the words were forced from her. "Then there is murder in him, too."

Robert's grasp loosened, awed by the strange look, but he faced her still.

"Tell me! Tell me what you did it for!" he said, with urgent appeal.

"Because they were hastening the end," she said, "and I could not have it. It is coming. I cannot stop it, but it shall not come yet."

"What is coming? What do you mean?" he said, his grasp tightening again. Patty shook it off.

"God's wrath and remembrance. One book is there; the only book you need, to learn what the end is for you, who are under the curse."

"Let God and his curses go; I care nothing for him nor for them," said Robert, fiercely. "You are mad, Mother, and I can't bear it any longer. There is nothing to do but leave you, and the time has come. This life is worse than death. I will not bear it."

"You must. You have no place in the world," Patty answered.

"Why not? What have I done that I cannot live? I have a place; or if I have not I can find one. Why do you always say these things?"

"Sit down," Patty said. "Be still. I must think."

Robert would have resisted, but something constrained him; the same power she had always had—to

silence, if not convince. But now he looked at her
half fiercely, half despairingly. Her eyes were fixed
on him, but as if she looked through him to something
beyond, and her hands clasped and unclasped nervously.
Her voice seemed to die away. The old pain came
sharp and bitter as if no years lay between it and her.
Then she spoke, rapidly and low.

Robert flushed as he listened; then grew deadly pale.
"Now go," she said at last. "Go, if you will. You
know the whole: why I am here; why I have wished
to keep the world away. Here or in the world you
suffer. Go; but remember, the iniquities of the father
are visited unto the third and fourth generation. You
are cursed with a curse."

Robert rose blindly and crept up the ladder to his
little loft. He did not yet take it in. He threw himself on the rough bed and pressed his hands on his
eyes and burning head. Through the chinks he could
see the stars shining. He stretched out his arms with
a vague feeling that they were nearer and kinder
than this inexorable God. Then hot, bitter tears
came. He buried his face in the pillow and shook with
the heavy sobs his mother must not hear. This father,
then, of whom he had dreamed, was a murderer; had
died under the hands of the common hangman. His
mother was right. There was no place for him in the
world. Who would not shrink from him, that knew
it? Cranstoun, even, rough as he was,—and Lockwood! Robert shivered. Yes, there was an end of all

that. No more books, no more of the letters that had helped everything. He would see him once and tell him it was all no use, that he must give up trying to make himself anything. To hide in the woods and forget that he ever wanted to leave them—that was all that remained. Then he went over his mother's story, step by step, till at last, worn with passion, he fell asleep.

For a moment, on awaking, he looked up with the old glad sense of abounding life. Only a moment, for like a flood the bitter knowledge swept over him. Silent, and with a look Patty had never seen, he went about that day and the next, and as she watched him she began to believe the warning effectual and his place to be still with her. In the boy's mind shame and sorrow were at war with the longing he felt to find Lockwood and pour it all out. Human pity and sympathy he must have, if only for one moment; but then he thought, "No; it is part of this curse that nobody will care; that everybody would shrink away. There is nothing to do but bear it."

By the third day this had become intolerable. Whatever happened, he must see Lockwood. Patty looked at him as he came down; his snow-shoes and pack slung over his shoulder.

"I am going away, Mother," he said. "I may come back, but I think not. Benoni will do all you need. You never have needed me."

Patty put out her hands as if to ward off a blow.

Then they dropped. How could he know the deep,
bitter yearning that rose over this son, put far from
her even before his life began? Robert came nearer
and looked at her, waiting for some sign. If she cared
for his pain even a moment it would make it easier.

"Do you care?" he said. "Have your ever cared?"

No answer. Benoni came forward with a sign of inquiry, which turned to distress as he saw the look on
Robert's face. The boy tried to smile, but tears were
coming. He brushed them away, laid his hand for a
moment on Benoni's shoulder, patted Cæsar, who
sought to follow him, and was gone.

Three days later, Lockwood, busy with a tray of
specimens which he was comparing, did not raise his
head as the office door opened softly. Indian visitors
were common, coming and going silently, but this
figure came to the table and stood waiting.

"Well," Lockwood said presently, then raised his
head. "What is it?—Robert! It can't be! It is!
Why, boy, how came you here?"

Lockwood saw that some unknown force had
moved the boy, and waited for the words that
seemed struggling and choking him. He locked the
door, drew two chairs near the fire, and, putting
Robert in one, sat down quietly. Robert's eyes had
the wild, strained look of one who has not slept, and
who, urged on by pain and bitter need, has come to
the end of endurance. He looked now silently into
Lockwood's face— a look which the young man could

not interpret—defiance, entreaty, almost mortal pain; then a dogged resolution, which, as he began to speak, forbade his looking down, but kept his eyes still fastened on the face of his friend, soon, he believed, to be parted from him by the new knowledge of what stood between. All the sharp sorrow of the long days since Patty had spoken, all the doubt and perplexity and utter wrecking of every plan and hope, he poured out as if for all the life before him no chance of such unburdening could ever come again.

The story ended. Then, dropping his head for one moment, Robert rose up and moved toward the door.

"What are you going to do, Robert?" Lockwood said huskily. Tears were in his eyes. He had almost broken down in listening; but Robert's face was pale and steady as he turned.

"I am going away somewhere. I don't know yet. I think, to the trappers beyond Marquette. There is no place for me anywhere."

"Your place is with me," Lockwood said, putting one arm about him. "Poor boy, do you think I could let you go? You must stay with me till this nightmare passes, and you can see how things look by daylight. You are almost dead with trouble. Wait till you are alive again before you try to understand it. Now come home with me."

Robert's eyes were fixed upon him; a look of intense searching.

"Then you don't hate me? You're willing to speak to me? You "——

His voice broke. Lockwood drew the youth toward him tenderly, as if he had been still a little child, and kissed his forehead, and Robert, who for a moment staggered and grew even paler, threw himself into a chair and laid his head on the table, shaking with the sobs he tried to suppress.

"I am ashamed," he said. "Oh, I am ashamed, but I did not know you would care. Now I can go easily."

Once more he started up, but Lockwood held him down.

"Not another word of that," he said. "You will go when I tell you to, and not before. I have nobody belonging to me, and I want you as much as you want me. God has brought us together, and till I tell you to go we will work together. Now we won't talk any more about it at present. Come."

No words could have ended protest so well as this formula under which Robert's life had grown. "We won't talk" had silenced so many phases of feeling that almost mechanically he rose up and followed Lockwood to his room in Searles's house. But now that the tension had relaxed he felt curiously weak and unsteady. The two long days in which he had pushed steadily on, unable to sleep, and lying by his camp-fire only for an hour or two, seemed like a dim dream. He had eaten but once, and then only a morsel to stay the sick faintness creeping over him, and now, as he stooped to

lay down his pack and snow-shoes, suddenly everything grew dark before him, and Lockwood, who sprang
forward, saw that he had fainted. Lockwood did all
that he could recall as necessary, but, when neither
rubbing nor the blast of cold air from the opened window availed, called to Searles, who had just come in
from the mine, and who as he hurried in, alarmed by
Lockwood's tone, looked for a moment at the prostrate
figure, staggered, and would have fallen himself had not
Lockwood caught him.

"My God!" he said. "It is Robert Saunders himself."

"I thought you had more sense, Searles," Lockwood
said angrily. "If you can't do anything call your wife.
I must get him on the bed."

Searles flushed.

"No need," he said. "My head swam a bit, and I
thought the boy was dead. What's the matter?"

"Half-starved, I should say," Lockwood answered.
"Ask your wife to warm some milk, and then go and
see if Dr. Barnett is in his office and can come round.
This mustn't go on."

"Well, I will say," began Mrs. Searles when told
what was required, "this house ain't a hospital nor
yet a hotel, and Mr. Lockwood can't turn us upside
down this way without my telling him what I think
about it. What with his miners, and his Ingins, and
his specimens behind the door and rubbing the paint
off every window-sill, and now some beggar calling for

hot milk, it's high time he should know what I think about it; and I'm going to speak my mind."

Mrs. Searles sped up the stairs; a small, nervous woman, with "faculty" written in every line of her sharp face and in the blue eyes which in youth might have been counted pretty, but which, wanting life and color, showed only the hardness common to a certain shade of blue in eyes; a shade in childhood—and even later on—popularly taken to mean amiability, dependence, modesty—all the feminine graces—but which with womanhood gains a steely quality; of all eyes the hardest, coldest, most unsympathetic. She stood now a little awed by this pale, still figure before her.

"He ain't dead, is he?" she said. "It will be the cap sheaf if you've got a dead man on your hands. I will say—"

"Bring me a cup of warm milk, please," Lockwood interrupted. "The boy has fainted from hunger. He is a friend of mine. Be quick, please."

Mrs. Searles shook her head as she descended the stairs, but hastened to heat the milk, and even looked with interest at the beautiful dark eyes which had opened at last, but heavily and uncertainly. "Go back, Ruth," she said, as the child, who had heard the call, came running and followed her; but Ruth did not heed, and pressed forward till she reached the foot of the bed, wondering why her father and Dr. Barnett and Lockwood, the people who made her little world, should all be here. So, as Robert came to full consciousness and tried to sit up, the face that first made itself plain to him was the wondering, pitying, half-frightened one of the child he had never forgotten.

"It's Ruth; it's little Ruth," he said, and shrank from the cup Lockwood held to his lips, his eyes still fixed upon her face.

"He'll do now," the doctor said. "All he needs is rest and food: not too much just yet. I'll come in again before night. He's had a great shock of some sort and must be quiet."

There was no need of enforcing this. Nature seemed to have taken the matter into her own motherly hands, and in the sleep which lasted for three days, only broken by an occasional rousing to take food, all the hard tension of nerve, the bitter stress of suppressed feeling, relaxed, and he awoke at last, weak but whole again, and ready for any work that lay before him.

Not entirely whole, either. The wound had cicatrized, but the old inflammation still burned underneath. The fact that his friend remained his friend carried healing and comfort, but only because that friend was better and nobler than all the rest of the world could such reception of his story be possible. A gulf lay between him and his kind. If Lockwood chose to cross it, it was the one blessing he could know; no other human being should ever be allowed the same right; and with the quiet inflexibility which had come to him from his mother he vowed that his life should be devoted to this one friend and such work as he could plan for him, and that no matter what temptation arose he would remember that he had been separated, once for all, from common interests and common ties. The fact that one knew it all, and in spite of knowledge accepted him, brought such comfort that to Lockwood—who saw that the despairing look was gone, and that the face held only quiet energy and an affection for himself almost passionate in its character—there was no suspicion that the old pain was still underneath.

Before a week had ended he wondered how he had done without the boy sq long, and as winter slowly gave place not to spring, for only the latter days of May had power to unlock the ice-bound lake, but to a short and fervent summer, passing quickly into a fleeting autumn soon lost in winter snows again, he found that he and not Robert had become the dependent one. No office that hands could do was left undone. Robert knew intuitively exactly what he wanted, and when; and watched with something of the anxiety and longing to satisfy that one sees in the eyes of a faithful dog. They worked side by side; for, as it chanced, at his coming the assistant engineer had left for a place offering larger pay, and, while the position was waiting for whoever might be sent, Robert took it, and by dint of hard study mastered every unfamiliar detail, carrying on the work so satisfactorily that no question of change arose.

To Searles the opportunity had come as if straight

from heaven. In the sixteen years since Robert Saunders's death the memory of Patty's words and face on that last day had never left him. He had married a young girl from a distant county, and at once gone West. She had known him as a wild, gay young fellow with a small property, and considered a good match by all her mates, and had no time to discover till after marriage that he had become an irritable, moody man, with long fits of silence against which her most energetic or caustic speech could make no headway. That some story lay behind this change she felt certain, but Searles had never admitted this, or even that he was changed in any degree.

"What do girls know about the young fellows that court them?" he said one day, as she complained that he did not seem the same. "It's our business to please you, and we fool round till it's done, but that has nothing to do with the way we live afterward. We see that you have a home and are looked after. Isn't that what you want?"

Hannah Searles was not given to analyzing either herself or other people very sharply. Narrow by nature, and made more narrow by limited education and utter lack of demonstration, whatever affection she had had been given to the gay, loud-talking, vociferous young man who had represented a broader outlook than she had ever known, and who had fallen violently in love with the delicate features and large blue eyes of this prim and even then somewhat angular maiden.

When his trouble came, and the friend with whom he had grown up went to a felon's death through the testimony he could not withhold, a sudden and permanent change came upon Searles. At first he determined to tell Hannah Bowen, who, living remote from the lake shore, had heard nothing, or if hearing had paid no attention to any details of the murder; but her wide-eyed astonishment and even shrinking, as he tried to discover how she would feel if any friend of hers had fallen into such trouble, silenced him. Girls could not understand, he concluded, and were not intended to; yet, as he saw how Robert leaned on Patty to the end, his own heart craved bitterly some rest for its own pain, and wondered if marriage would make it any easier to tell the whole. His old occupations and amusements grew hateful to him. To marry, to break away from all old associations and begin a new life, became his strongest longing, and within a few weeks of Robert's death he had left for the West; ending at last at Lake Superior, where his old knowledge of mining gave him a position as manager, which he had filled for years, gradually becoming an authority among mining men.

Untrained, but of excellent natural ability, he gave himself to study bearing on his own calling, and lost himself as far as possible in hard work. With a more loving woman the time of confession and outpouring might have come. But Hannah Searles, absorbed in saving money and in a state of chronic bitterness at her husband's laxness in such matters,

had no conception of any deeper needs than three
meals a day, carefully kept clothes and a spotlessly
neat house. The birth of Ruth, three years after marriage, had been a serious interruption, and the baby
would have known very little of baby life but for her
father, to whom from the first moment of consciousness she seemed to turn with an instinct which had
grown with her growth, till now the pair seemed to
live only for one another. All the repression and pain
of those years of work, all the craving and uneasy longing and vague hope of better days and of atonement,
seemed to find expression in this quiet child, who followed him first with eyes, and then with tiny, tottering
feet, and was never content save when close to him.

"Well, I will say, I never expected to see a man
fool so over a child," Mrs. Searles ejaculated day after
day, as Searles sat down to his books with the little
figure in his arms, or playing at his feet; and eleven
years had had no power to modify this astonishment.
Ruth looked at her mother quietly and considerately
as her sharp voice rose and fell in the old complaints:
obeyed her without question or comment in all matters
not relating to her father, and was growing up into
deft and dainty ways. But no stress of housekeeping
urgency could keep her from him when his day's work
was ended; and the two talked hours together, to the
astonishment and disgust of Mrs. Searles, who saw no
use in such waste of time, and considered that entire
infatuation held them both,

CHAPTER XIV.

ITH Robert's first coming, a longing possessed Searles to keep the boy with him, and, in the five years since the light falling on him from the bit of sky above the shaft had shown with startling distinctness features long since hidden under ground, he had planned many methods of bringing this about. Now the time had come, and whatever he could do for the boy should be done. Ruth, when a little older, should know the whole, and the hope grew up that in a not distant future her life might be his atonement to the dead.

"I will say," Mrs. Searles broke out one day in her usual formula, as if her life ordinarily were one of iron repression, and the assertion necessary to prevent entire obliteration, "I will say, that it does look curious, the way you take to this boy. One might think you'd known him before, the way you an' Ruth cotton to him. I ain't so free with strangers, and he not speaking unless he takes a notion. Did you know any of his folks?"

Searles flushed hotly.

"I knew his father once," he said, after a pause. "When I was a boy."

"If you'd said his mother you'd hit it nearer," said Mrs. Searles with a curious look. "I'd like to know who she was. Robert!" she called to Robert passing through the room, and so hastily Searles could not have checked her if he would, "Robert! where did your folks come from?"

"I haven't any but mother and Benoni," he said with a surprised look.

" Where's your father?"

" He is dead," Robert answered, and went on, unheeding the next remark.

" Seems to me you needn't clip it off so short. Folks that ain't ashamed of their own have more to say."

"That will do, Hannah," Searles said sternly. "If the boy does not choose to talk, let him alone. It's none of our affair where he came from. Ask no more questions."

"Humph!" was all the answer made, but a suspicion had entered her mind which grew and strengthened from day to day. Searles's evident affection for the boy, and equally evident intention to help him in all possible ways, could have but one foundation. She studied Robert's face, seeking some shadow of resemblance to the man she had determined to be his father, and took every opportunity of questioning as to his mother's life, past and present. That these opportunities rarely came whetted her curiosity only the more, and Searles little knew what web of ingenious possibility had been woven by the quiet jealousy of a woman of small passion, but of vindictive and narrow feeling, who came at last to regard herself as a victim and to look upon Lockwood as an active agent in the deception practiced upon her. His money, however, was an important item, and so far as she could feel genuine friendliness for any one she had felt it for him in spite of his erratic ways. Lockwood and Searles had met in a trip of the former, when a boy, up Lake Champlain. They had spent a week or two in the woods together, and Lockwood had never forgotten the hearty young fellow who had given him his first lessons in woodcraft, and with whom he had always kept up some slight intercourse, till, accepting his present position, he had taken up quarters with his old acquaintance. The change in Searles had not only puzzled but startled him, but he assigned it to money-troubles and the wearing, aggressive temper of his wife. At moments, he had fancied Searles upon the point of confiding in him; but as yet he had never spoken, and their interests centered about their daily work and the child for whom Lockwood cared, next to Robert. All these details Hannah Searles knew, but in her groping about for connections between the three she imagined that her husband must at some time have told Lockwood the story of his youth, and of the causes which had wrought the change whose existence he persistently denied. These causes she would some day discover. Positive knowledge had not yet come; and, though aggrieved, she could make no definite charges and must simply bide her time, ready to act, and bent upon retaliation should retaliation prove possible. Robert she could have liked, for he helped rather than hindered her scheme of life, but she drew back constantly, determining to be rid of him at the first opportunity.

Meanwhile she found solace in her round of work and in the increasing bank account, already sufficient to make them persons of consideration in the little village given over to copper, wherein every man and woman looked forward to investing in mining shares, and even if this crowning height was never reached felt a sense of personal property in the great smelting furnaces or the huge steam crushers.

In this copper region there was little of the beauty which surrounded Robert's old home. An artist would have reveled in the clear coloring of these copper-hills —the myriad shadings of the many ores, the masses of rock rising sheer from the blue water, and the background of somber pines, only lightened here and there by feathery white birches. Compact and bustling as the little settlement was, over all brooded a sense of loneliness—a part of the great lake stretching like another ocean far beyond any vision, and beating always with a measured throb against the cliffs. Here and there were inlets where the water lapped softly on reaches of white sand, and into one of these emptied a little river, which, though quiet and deep on its way to

the north, broke here into flying foam, and tumbled
from rock to rock, a sheer fall at last of many feet.
Down these rapids the more venturous Indian boys
sometimes shot to a flat rock rising high, just before
the final fall, to which they sprang, letting the light
canoe go on with the flood, and float, bottom up, in the
inlet till they swam out and righted it. It was dangerous play, but Robert, who watched them, had been more
than once tempted to try it, and Ruth, who had been
taught by her father to manage a canoe, to the consternation and general outrage of all her mother's sense
of what a girl should and should not do, watched it
too, with a thrill of apprehension yet of delight, as the
lithe figures made the final spring and stood in safety
while the canoe whirled to seeming destruction below.

Indians came and went at will; some from the Indian
settlement at Sault St. Marie, some from the interior
country; and most of them dirty, degraded and drunk-
en—this condition the only link between themselves
and the equally drunken and degraded whites, who had
imparted thus much of civilization and no more. But
now and then from the Minnesota border of the great
lake came a band of the original lake Indians—stately
men, with magnificent chests, deepened and broadened
by a lifetime with canoe and paddle, and who stayed
only long enough to sell their furs and return to the
region from which as yet the white man's whisky was
shut out. There were moments when Robert remembered his wild life, and, with the thought of what his

future must be, was tempted to join them, and cast off forever the burden entailed upon him if he remained with his own kind.

In these months, during which he had worked steadily and quietly, the last trace of boyhood had disappeared.

"You were born at least ten years old," Lockwood sometimes said laughingly. "Certainly no one would dream you were less than twenty-five, Robert, and there are moments when I should say twice that. You must aim to grow young as carefully as I to grow old."

Robert smiled the grave smile which only came occasionally, but which had all the beauty—the clear lighting up as if from within—that his mother's face had known in her girlhood. But a curious likeness was growing up between them. Features and coloring were the father's, but the mother's sad and bitter soul seemed now to look from the boy's eyes, and to forbid the old joyous content. Of the past he never spoke, and Lockwood, who noticed the sorrowful expression that came over the face in repose, dreaded to intensify by argument any morbidness still remaining. The old eagerness came constantly to the surface in study. He worked with an intensity that knew no relaxation, and bade fair to gain all that any college course in books could have given him.

At times Lockwood wondered if such a course and the resulting contact with those of his own age might not drive away the shadows about him, but trusted at last to time and life to make problems plain. Ruth would help, for in spite of rebuff Ruth followed and clung to him as she had never clung to anyone but her father. Robert was never harsh. His eyes softened as she came near, and evidently he would gladly have given himself up to the charm of the little maid's presence. As months passed he did so more and more, but always as if some veil were between. Ruth considered him gravely, but made no comment. Often, though, as she sat by her father going over lessons, or entering into long discussions over her small theories of life, she called Robert, and the three talked together as if much of the same age and with the same interests. As they talked, Hannah Searles looked up from her work and studied the faces of man and boy with an intentness that often made itself felt, and Robert turning suddenly would find her eyes fixed upon him with a question in them he could never understand.

Of his home Robert never spoke. He had written to Cranstoun, a few weeks after reaching Houghton, that he wanted him to find out just how Benoni and his mother were, but it was not till summer that an Indian runner had come one day into the office and drawn a blotted and soiled envelope from his muskrat pouch. Probably the first letter that Cranstoun had ever written, it bore traces not only of bodily toil but much mental suffering in its composition. Lines were smeared out as if with a broad thumb; words were spelled in several methods and all left, as if intended that Robert should make such selection as best pleased him, and the first laugh Lockwood had heard since his coming broke out as the crooked letters were deciphered. Translated, it read thus:

"Dere Robert: ime glad you are of. i went up and tha are al well and sed nothing. I ased for you and yure muther sed you was gone and I cud not get more out of her. Benonee wants to go and see yu. Do you want him to? I rekkon I shall cum miself some time.
"Yure tru friend and welwisher   JAMES CRANSTOUN."

Lockwood looked at the boy's face, still gleaming with merriment, yet even as he looked settling into the old, sad lines. The time had come for words he had longed to speak, yet checked, fearing they might do more harm than good.

"Let us have a walk," he said. "I want one more bit of ore for that empty corner in my tray, and we'll hunt it up."

CHAPTER XV.

HE bit of ore was soon secured, and the pair strolled on past the furnaces and out on the Point stretching far into the lake, to a group of pines at the end, under which they often sat on summer evenings. The sun had gone down but the clouds still glowed, crimson and deepest gold, and the lake gave back the rich coloring and the sheen of the copper hills, each one clear and sharp in the depth below.

Robert threw himself on the ground and tossed aside his hat, and Lockwood followed his motion and, leaning against a tree, looked off to the hills. A cool wind swept down from them, rippling the lake and swaying the fringe of the bushes about the point, and Robert, before whom a picture of his old haunt by the inlet at home had come, said suddenly,

"I wonder if Cranstoun went to the inlet, and if it all looks the same. Seven months can't have changed it much."

"Good soul!" Lockwood said. "He has been a good friend to you from the beginning."

"Yes," Robert answered, absently, "I know it, but he wouldn't have been if he'd known."

"Robert," Lockwood said, "it isn't possible that you are still dwelling on that trouble. I thought you had put it all away. Can't you begin to believe that God has something better for you than a curse?"

"I wish I could stop believing in him at all," Robert burst out. "If that might be, I could begin to live. But here I am in his grip and it never lets go. 'Cursed with a curse,' my mother said. 'Go if you will, but you are cursed with a curse and it will follow you.' It does follow me. There are minutes when I look up and think God is and must be kind; when the old life rises and I could run and shout from pure gladness; and then it all shuts down, and I see that sooner or later I shall do some desperate thing, or fail in what I most want, because that curse is on me. It's a hand to hand fight. I'm bound to win. I will win if mortal man can stand out against God; and yet, Dwight—it's bound to conquer. I wish I might die."

"But if God were fighting with instead of against you," said Lockwood, after a pause in which their eyes had met in a long look of questioning sadness; "if this feeling of yours is from the strange spirit of evil that knows your weakest side, and plays upon it, and your longing to conquer is from God, who never has blighted and never will blight a single human life past recovery; what then?"

"You know better," said Robert, hastily. "'The sins of the father'—have you forgotten?"

"No, and I could not forget, for I see its truth every

day. They are visited, but not as you think. There is
not an inherited appetite or passion or vice that cannot be fought down; and the very fact that you are
hindered with an inheritance for which you are in no
degree responsible gives you an added claim on God's
love. With the temptation comes an even more
open way of escape than is granted to less weighted
souls. The very knowledge that you are weighted
puts you more on your guard. Your struggle against
such odds calls to your aid every force that God sends
into the human soul. But, Robert, you are not burdened as you think. I have gone over and over
every detail you told me, and that murder was no result of deliberate sin or unregulated passion—indeed, it was no murder, as I see it. Even your
mother believes it an accident, and has told you
so. Your life had begun to grow before this tragedy
came, and all that love could do to give you the best it
had, was done. You were not sealed with the seal of
a drunken, or brutal, or vicious love. You have read
enough to understand that such birth is to appetites and
tendencies against which many struggle in vain, but
even with them I have known training and self-denial
bring conquest and a good life. You have no such
antecedents. Your mother must be a beautiful soul,
fatally warped. Everyone belonging to her seems to
have been good and true. Your father, she says herself, was generous, tender and noble, in spite of wild-
ness, and died patient and accepting death as God's

will. The burden you carry comes not from him, but
from the sad soul of your mother, who perverted every
word of comfort and interpreted literally a verse
meant not as a curse but as an awful warning to sin-
ful men that the consequences of their sin must be
visited on innocent heads. The drunken father sends
an idiot child into the world. Is that child responsible? And can't you believe that, bitter as the fate seems
to us, it is only God's warning to men to use reason
and prevent such possibilities? There is compensation
for every such soul when another life is reached, and
the poor, hampered, prisoned mind comes to the only
real life. There is not one of us that has not some
special weakness or temptation to sin. There is not
one of us who cannot so order his life that that very
sin may be his constant spur to endeavors, that at last
will bring a fruition which the less tempted and struggling life could never know. Strength made perfect in
weakness—that is it. Your temptation is of another sort.
You are ten times freer than I from low desires and
strong passions, but you have first been made faithless
as to God's love, and then taught to believe a lie. It
is a lie. You are *not* under a curse. If spirits returned
to us, your own father would say to you this moment:
'The love that is waiting for you in the heart of God
is deeper and stronger than all the human love the
very happiest life can know. I found it and believed
it, and rest in it now. Give up doubt; take your portion, and do the work to which you are called.'"

Robert had half risen, and leaned forward, his eyes fixed on the young man's face. Lockwood spoke as if moved by some interior force, and every power of will and thought in him reached out to this imprisoned nature, longing for the light, which waited only till his own hand should open the windows of his soul and see the clear shining, flooding the whole world about him. He drew a deep, long breath, and laid one hand on Lockwood's, who looked eagerly at him. Then he said :

" I could almost believe you, Dwight. It has never seemed so possible before. But only the other day I read that book of yours—'Galton.' I did not understand it all, I think, but I understood enough to find what heredity means, and it is useless to deny its power."

" I do not deny it," Lockwood answered. " I *know* its power. But I look at it, not as God's curse, but as God's school, for his world. The time is coming when every law that governs it will be so understood that idiots and lunatics and hopeless cripples cannot be born. Even if legislative enactment does not hinder it—and it will in extreme cases—men and women will come to such knowledge that their own common sense will be law sufficient. There will always be the residuum of brutes and scoundrels, and these must be dealt with by law. But the world is struggling up into light. Each generation has a little more wisdom than the last; each generation is approaching, no mat-

ter how faintly, the day of purer manners—nobler
laws. You and I will not see it, but we can work for
it; and we work not under a hard, relentless task-
master, but under the King in his beauty. The whole
creation groaneth and travaileth together, but the end
is deliverance from pain, and a glorious new life. We
have glimpses of it now. Every noble thought—every
true life—is the promise of better things to come.
Christ came for this, and trod all ·that weary way for
no other end. Follow him, take the strength that
comes to all who seek to do his will, and your trouble
will end and life begin. How shall I make you believe
it, Robert? "

Robert was silent, but he still held his friend's hand
and the sadness had given way to a look of earnest
questioning.

" Promise me one thing," Lockwood said at last.
" I do not expect you to be convinced at once. But
do not shut yourself up with your own brooding
thoughts. Talk them out and we will try and find
answers. If you love me at all, Robert, do this for
me. Promise."

Robert hesitated, but Lockwood's eyes held a com-
pelling force he had never felt before, and he answered
at last, slowly and solemnly, "I promise."

"Thank God!" was in Lockwood's heart, but he
only grasped the boy's hand more tightly and then
rose up. The wedge had entered, if ever so lightly,
and there was hope that quiet and persistent urgency

would at last open this hidden spring of bitter waters
to sunshine and sweet air.

As they left the Point and passed up the village
street, Ruth and her mother came toward them on
their way to Thursday evening prayer-meeting. Searles
himself was away, testing some specimens from a
new lead, and at such times Mrs. Searles seized the
opportunity to give the religious instruction with
which her husband never meddled.

Mrs. Searles was herself a Methodist, finding more
stimulant for her cold and limited nature in this form
than in any other, and going constantly to prayer-
meeting, and love-feast, and any and every church ex-
ercise. Ruth shrank from the noise and confusion with
which such meetings usually ended, and preferred the
decorous order found in the little Episcopal church
set deep in pines, and with more pretension to beauty
than the square boxes known as Presbyterian and
Methodist places of worship. A small proportion of
the miners, and these chiefly Welsh and South of England men, came to the latter, but the great mass
seemed beyond all such influences, and gave Sunday to
drinking, boating, fighting—anything that could wile
away the idle hours. Among these men Lockwood
had gone in the beginning of his life at Houghton, his
hearty, genial manner taking him into places from
which a less popular man would have been rebuffed,
and he had worked in quiet ways; earning for himself
the title of infidel and heathen from the over-zealous

Methodist minister, who could see but one way into the kingdom of heaven, and that narrower even than the path in which he was an accredited guide. The miners; the remnant of Indians still hovering about the settlement; the French half bloods who filled the little Catholic church on the bluff, and who between the intervals of confession stole indiscriminately and with an equanimity never affected by discovery or conviction, made up a field of operations into which Lockwood plunged at first with the enthusiasm and faith of earnest youth. Five years had not quenched this ardor, but had taught him to limit his effort. A new man had come to the Methodists—middle-aged, energetic, and with a knowledge of human nature gained in his life in a great city as a workingman, long before his call to preach was heard and followed, and who did not hesitate to announce that there were men they met daily, so dead in sins, or so seared and stupid, that "God didn't want them and even the devil wouldn't have them." This was the Rev. Thomas Brown.

"You've got to draw the line of work somewhere," he said, one day in the office, as Lockwood ordered off a hulking half-blood who had been telling of some wrong done by a miner, and demanding satisfaction from the Company. "I may exhort that fellow till Gabriel blows, and what is there to get hold of? First, he's cased in superstition, and thinks I'm on the high road to hell because I'm a Protestant, and under that is ignorance thick enough to hinder the wisest words from getting

in, and under that is his own animal nature : a set of
sharp instincts and passions.   There isn't soul enough
in ten of them to make up anything big enough to
save.   What do I do then?   Fret over it?   Not I!   I
turn to the man or woman I can reach and spend my
energy on them.   If the Lord thinks anything is to be
done with such as they, he'll open the way and I
shall know it.   I could make more headway with any
ten Injuns than I could with one of those fellows."

"Very shocking doctrine," said Mr. Gray, severely,
"very shocking from any one, but more so from one
who claims to preach the Gospel.   I admit there are
degrees in the power to understand, but it is your
business and mine to preach, in season and out of
season."

"That pesky text has knocked more good work
endways than you could shake a stick at," said Mr.
Brown, vigorously.

Mr. Gray shivered. Such ádjectives were demolishing
and outraging and should not be countenanced, and he
looked appealingly at Lockwood, whose face was quietly
good humored as usual and who gave no sign of any leaning toward either.   "I tell you," Mr. Brown pursued,
walking up and down energetically, "you'll never get
at these people till you learn to humor them and take
their season and not yours.   Sometimes I wish the
Bible wasn't so common.   It's an old story, and it gets
read, so many chapters or verses like so many pills, or
it's made a bugaboo of, and the live facts in it are all

swaddled and swathed till they can't stir. I have a good mind sometimes to say it ought to be suppressed a bit—nobody read it till they're a certain age, only have bits of it and be taught how to take it. I've done it now," he added, as the little minister swept up hat and cane and fled as if from the adversary himself. "I'll go after him. I didn't mean to hurt his feelings."

Robert smiled as the pair disappeared. Such endings were common. Lockwood laughed and turned to his work again, in no way disturbed. The office had long been neutral ground for these opposing forces, Dr. Barnet adding another element, as he ran in to report his day's work and growl over the thick-headedness of the miners and the miners' wives. Robert listened to all with an avidity that the every-day boy, brought up among churches and ministers, could never have felt: compared statements and beliefs, and from the mass of argument and often mutual vituperation was gradually constructing his own system. In the meantime, though labored with by both the Methodist and Presbyterian representatives, who saw in his quiet reserve the possibility of a future theological student, he drew back from both, and, in the rare times when he entered a church at all, preferred the stately and venerable form of the Episcopal service, which he followed with a serious pleasure that gave Mr. Gray strongest hopes of an ultimate convert. Now and then Ruth and he went together, but always under protest from Mrs.

Searles, who complained bitterly that Ruth was growing up to cross her mother wherever she could.

As the child grew older, standing already on the threshold of girlhood, and with no childish ways save the fondling reserved for her father, a certain sense of something she had lost troubled the shallow pool of Hannah Searles's nature. She saw no cause for repentance over any lack in herself, yet looked on with a jealousy she could not suppress at the good comradeship growing daily stronger between father and daughter. She interrupted their work or talk whenever possible; found unexpected tasks for Ruth, or brought her own complaints into the conversation, till Searles one day turned upon her:

"What's come over you, Hannah, I don't know, but I should say you were bound I shouldn't have a quiet minute with Ruth. Now understand: evening's my time, and not to be touched. You do as you please in the day-time when I'm not on hand; when I am, let us alone."

Robert winced as he heard the sharp, decisive words, and Mrs. Searles was silent from pure astonishment. As a rule, she went her own way absolutely. Searles might be irritable and moody, but he never interfered with her plans, so that the rare decision of tone was more effective when it did come. She had found herself powerless to influence him against Robert, and her own fear and suspicion had settled into a dislike too quiet to take any active measures, and simply waiting opportunity for venting itself. Since Mr. Brown's coming and his interest in the boy a new possibility had dawned. Robert's conversion would, in one so studious, lead to the ministry. Once induce him to become a preacher, and not only was he removed from her own life but the cause of religion gained an advocate such as did not every day go over to it. To Robert's surprise she had become an exhorter, urged him to go to meetings, laid tracts of warning or entreaty in his room, and adopted all the methods known to her line of thought, growing only more indignant as he quietly put them aside and went his accustomed way.

"I won't have him in the house," she had said again and again; but, as no valid reason could be given for turning him out, was forced still to wait, growing only more eager and intent upon her end as weeks passed into months and still no sign of accomplishment became visible.

CHAPTER XVI.

N the evening in question, when Mrs. Searles with Ruth met Robert and Lockwood, she stopped. Something in the boy's face struck her as new and surprising. He touched his hat with the courtesy he was learning from Lockwood, whose fashions of manner he copied with a faith that none could be so perfect, and Ruth looked up at him with the feeling, often filling her little mind, that the world could never hold any one so beautiful or so much to be admired. His life-time in the open air had done away with all the angularity usually attendant upon such sudden growth, and his absorption in one idea shut off the possibility of much self-consciousness—that fruitful parent of all awkwardness—so that motion and bearing were free and unconstrained; and even the throwing aside of hunting shirt and moccasins and the adoption of thoroughly civilized dress had not had power to develop any of that latent boorishness which sometimes lies in hiding till brought to light by unaccustomed garb. Robert, like Lockwood, looked thoroughly the gentleman, and Mrs. Searles was too much a woman not to feel a certain pleasure as the tall figure turned and walked on with them.

"'Tain't to be wondered at Searles takes to him," she said to herself. "If he'd tell me the truth I'd do well by him myself, for there ain't a young fellow like him anywhere round. But I won't be deceived and put upon. I'll find out, if I have to face the woman myself, wherever she is."

Robert had taken Ruth's hand and walked on, answering her flow of talk. At the door leading up to the room where meetings were held he turned, but Mrs. Searles stopped him.

"Come," she said; "it's a long while since you've been in with me. 'Twon't hurt you. Come in."

Robert hesitated. Still full of the feeling brought out by his talk with Lockwood, he was in no mood for the vociferousness and ejaculations he had heard so often that with closed eyes he could tell from whom each word came, but Ruth held him.

"I don't like it any better than you," she whispered. "Come, just for once."

Robert followed, and ascended the stairs to the barn-like room over what had been the principal store, used instead of the church because more easily lighted. The building had been put up hurriedly and in the unsubstantial way not confined to new settlements, and now and then it had been suggested that it was not perfectly safe. Lately the walls of the building next door had been taken down, and as the congregation

settled into their places this evening it seemed to Robert
for a moment that a peculiar tremor went through the
floor. It was gone in a moment, and the meeting went
on as usual till, as the customary round of prayers
ended and the minister stepped forward for the evening exhortation, Robert, who had sat lost in thought
over all that Lockwood had said, suddenly sprang up,
and seizing Ruth rushed toward the door. What
strange, warning power had moved him he could never
tell, but as he passed through it and stood panting
upon the stairs, Ruth clinging to him in silent fright,
there was a crashing sound, and then a terrible cry, as
the hundred men, women and children suddenly were
buried in the mass of heavy flooring and plastering in
which they were struggling. The floor had given way
and the staircase itself was tottering. Robert, still holding Ruth, made but a leap to the bottom and stood without, expecting to see the whole building fall. From every
point people came running, and quickly men were at
work, dragging away beams and lifting out terrified
men or fainting women.

"I must help," he said. "Ruth, can you go home
alone?"

"I must stay here," she answered. "I will be still;
but I must stay, for Mother is there."

"Run home and have everything ready," Robert
said, as she slid from his arms and stood trembling
but quiet. "She may be badly hurt. Can you go,
Ruth?"

Ruth turned and sped silently away, and Robert, filled with a sick dread of what he might find, went forward. But as senses returned to those who had fainted, only bruises, and in many cases no sign even of them, were discernible. The large proportion were unhurt, but a few at the center of the room were still held by the weight of flooring, and screams and groans told only too well that here the most harm had been done. Mrs. Searles was the last one taken out. A beam lay directly across her, and the moving it required most anxious care lest others should be dislodged and fall also. Robert helped lift her to the improvised stretcher and carry her to her own home; then returned to the spot where the minister, though with broken arm and a cut in the forehead from which blood had streamed till some one bound it up with a handkerchief, had staid till assured none were left in the building, and as he was led away to his own house protested that he could wait and that others needed a doctor more than he.

Beyond a few fractured bones and many cuts and bruises no serious harm had been done, and among them all only one was likely to feel the effects for the rest of her time in the world. The crushed knee had at first seemed the only injury, but, as days went on and Hannah Searles lay with little sensibility to anything passing about her, Dr. Barnet shook his head. Some internal injury there most evidently was, but early winter had come before its nature could be rec-

ognized or dealt with. Consciousness came back slowly. Then the power of sharp and irritable speech and
ability to move the hands and arms; but, before that
day, all but herself knew that beyond this her active
life in the world had ended once for all.

"She ought to be told," Dr. Barnet said, but Searles
shook his head.

"It would kill her. Wait awhile," he answered to
each fresh urging.

"The ways of men are past finding out," Dr. Barnet
said, as he went one day from her bedside to Lockwood's office. "I suppose there isn't a sharper tongue
in Houghton, or a more uncomfortable man than she
has made Searles in that way, and yet he hangs over
her as if she were a suffering saint or martyr. Personally, I should say her death was all that was
needed to release not only herself but everybody
connected with her from suffering; but I don't
know."

"It's going to develop a new set of faculties in
Ruth," Lockwood answered. "She was an unpracti-
cal little body : deft, when she fixed her mind upon a
thing, but disliking detail. I see the change already,
and perhaps the trouble has come just for that—to turn
her dreamy temperament into a more practical channel, while teaching the mother that there is a life with
which work has nothing to do."

"All very well," said the doctor, irritably. "But I
don't see any advantage in smashing up a whole con-

gregation to keep one girl from wool-gathering. That's what it amounts to."

"I'm not so sure," said Lockwood, laughing. "Brown has won the admiration of a lot of rough fellows who have watched him going about, with his broken arm, comforting and helping with even more energy than usual. They're ready to swear by him now, so that any chasm in his congregation is likely to be filled. But Mrs. Searles won't last. She'll fret herself out of the world."

"No such good luck," returned Dr. Barnet, still moody. "She may fret other people, but she has the vitality of twenty and will lie there to old age for all I see. Objection to it on my part is unprofessional, I know. I'm only speaking for the child's sake."

"Robert," Mrs. Searles said that night, as he came to change her position, his strong arms seeming to accomplish it more easily than her husband's. She had turned to him from the beginning of consciousness, and begged him daily to sit where she could see him. Robert had met her wish, but looked up often uneasily to find her eyes fixed on him with the curious look he could never interpret. To-night she held his sleeve for a moment as he turned her.

"Robert, I can't make Ruth answer me. When am I going to get up?"

Robert was silent.

"What do you mean by keeping still? You don't mean—you don't mean I ain't going to get up at all?"

Still silence.

"Answer me," she said, fiercely. "You, standing there, laughing at me, more than likely! Do you mean I'm not to get up at all?"

"I don't suppose you ever will," Robert said. "I wish you hadn't asked me. The doctor knows."

"The doctor doesn't know," she said, passionately. "He's a fool. I'll have some one else. There's a healing medium at Marquette; I'll send for him. Do you think I'll lie here and let you and your schemes go on? Do you think I don't know what you are and what you mean? Oh, you're very quiet, but I understand. You'll wheedle every one and then step in and take the money I've saved for Ruth. You think you'll be master here some day. Wait till I'm well, and you'll see! And as for your mother, I'll find means yet to punish her—a miserable"——

A fit of hysterical crying interrupted the torrent that would have come. Robert listened in deepest amazement. What could she know of him? Had Lockwood incautiously dropped any word she could pervert, or was it only a sick fancy? Searles, who had come in, listened in equal astonishment.

"Go away," he said. "She's out of her mind. Just let it go, Robert."

Lockwood, to whom he went after deliberating whether he should speak or not, made the same answer.

"Of course she knows nothing," he said, "and could

know nothing. You must expect fancies from her, but never answer them. All knowledge of your trouble is yours and mine alone."

Reassured, yet still perplexed, Robert looked for further developments, but the invalid had settled into a sullen silence, and for days gave no sign of interest or attention. What conflict was going on in her mind only God could know; what struggle to adjust herself to these bitter conditions—what wild rebellion against fate. No word indicated the storm of rage she felt at moments, and, as days passed, she looked only more worn and haggard. Robert kept away except when called to lift her, and she avoided his eyes. Mr. Brown came daily to pray with her, and left, shaking his head.

"There's a mysterious work going on," he said, "and the Lord knows whether he or the devil's to conquer. I fear—I fear much—it's going to be the devil."

CHAPTER XVII.

 FORTNIGHT of this brooding silence had passed. Searles watched his wife with a patient care that would have been pronounced impossible to one of his irritable temper, coming straight to her bedside from his daily work. One neighbor and another volunteered help, but their presence, or even the knowledge that they were in the house, seemed to irritate and disturb the invalid. Lockwood and Robert arranged to take their meals next door, that as little work as possible might fall upon Ruth. In this remote and primitive region the "hired girl" was an almost unknown species. The hotel in summer labored under the burden of two or three, brought up for the season from Detroit, and a few of the richer families struggled to retain their own; but for the most part each household depended upon itself and the occasional assistance of two or three of the French-Canadian women, strong and active, who made nothing of walking two or three miles in and out, doing a heavy day's scrubbing, and ending with their own house-work. One of

these, Annette Leroy, had been Mrs. Searles's dependence in emergencies, and would have stayed now had
not the patient roused long enough to order her out
of the room.

"Ruth can do what's wanted," she said, "and what
she can't may stay undone. I won't have folks poking
round among my things, and you may as well understand it first as last."

Searles made no answer beyond a soothing "Well,
she sha'n't stay," but ten days later walked into the
office with an open letter in his hand.

"Lockwood," he said, with a most unaccustomed
smile still lighting his face, "I've got a letter from an
an old friend of yours. Do you remember Tempy
Perkins, that taught the district school that summer
you was at our house? She boarded there too."

"I am not likely to forget her," Lockwood said with
an answering smile. "I remember that when the
butcher failed to come she killed a sheep and dressed
it; that she punished a boy six feet high and brought
him to terms, and danced with him next night at the
harvest-ball in the barn. I remember the tightness of
her curls. I can see her eyes snap this moment.
What about her?"

"She's a sort of cousin—my mother's cousin,"
Searles said, "and not very well-to-do. I knew she
wasn't married, and when I found Hannah would never
stir round again, I wrote to find out if she was free,
and if she'd come out here. She hasn't lost any time.

She rented her little house just as it stood, and is on the way now. I didn't suppose she'd be so quick, and I haven't spoken to Hannah. Would you do it now, or wait till she comes?"

"Wait, by all means. She will not have time to think up objections, and it may rouse her. There is no doubt about the rousing," he added, as Searles went out. "If Miss Tempy retains any of the characteristics of fifteen years ago she would rouse the dead. She sung ballads in those days—old revolutionary ones, learned from her grandfather—and I remember sitting a whole rainy afternoon helping her string apples while she sung 'Lovewell's Fight' and a dozen others in a thin, high voice that goes through my head now. I think she'll be mistress of the situation."

Three days later the steamer-whistle sounded, and Searles and Lockwood—the former with some misgivings—went down to the wharf, reaching there just in time to see a stout, startlingly erect, middle-aged woman step ashore. The pipe-stem curls were there—iron-gray now—and the snapping black eyes, which had, however, a very kindly look, only a trifle obscured by the general energy of her expression and manner.

"Pleased to see you, Cousin Benjamin," she said kindly, after one keen look at the changed face. "There ain't no hurry. We'll have time enough to get acquainted again."

Lockwood put out his hand. "I thought I knew you, but I can't just place you," she said slowly, looking at him intently. "Lawful heart! It's that good-for-nothing Dwight Lockwood! How come you here?"

"Engineer for the Bascom Smelting Works, and very much at your service," he said laughing. "I haven't felt so young for fifteen years. You have a good memory, Miss Tempy. You'll need it, and all your other good qualities, in the work you've come to do."

"H'm!" was Miss Tempy's only answer, as she turned to watch Searles, who had taken her checks and was overseeing the piling of her old-fashioned luggage —hair-trunks and wooden chests—on a cart. Her quick-roving eyes took in everything. By the time they reached the door Lockwood felt she knew almost as much of the village as he, for her equally quick tongue had kept up an incessant run of questions. Ruth looked at her apprehensively.

"Come still," she said. "We mustn't rouse Mother."

"Tell me exactly about the hull on't," said Miss Tempy, who declined to sit, and stood with her bonnet on, till Searles had given every detail of the two months since the accident.

Miss Tempy took off her bonnet as the story ended, folded her shawl, smoothed down her curls, and turned toward the sick-room.

"Part o' my business 's been nursing," she said, "and there ain't a crank nor a turn in folks 't I ain't used to. I'll just go in now."

"Dinner is ready," said Ruth. "Not a very good

one, because I don't know much yet; but won't you
eat dinner before you go in?"

"Guess not," was the answer, as with the word she
stepped inside the sick-room. Ruth and her father followed, in dread of the result; but Miss Tempy's manner had changed from almost aggressive energy to
perfect quiet.

Mrs. Searles lay with closed eyes. If she had heard
the strange voice she gave no sign; but now, as all
came near her bed, she opened her eyes slowly, then
fastened them upon the new-comer.

"Who are you?" she said.

"Temperance Perkins — Ben's mother's second-
cousin."

"What are you here for?"

"Because I'm a regular nurse and can look after
things."

Mrs. Searles's eyes flashed with something of their
old fire.

"Folks that come without an invitation," she said,
"needn't look for much ceremony. You can just put
on your things and march."

"Mother!" Ruth said, distressed; but Miss Tempy's
face was unmoved.

"We'll talk about that when you're some better,"
she said. "I calkilate to stay a spell, anyhow."

"You've heard about Tempy," Searles said—"she
that nursed Mother in her last sickness, and Father,
too. She's a master hand at it."

The words were unfortunate.

"I'm not going to be nursed out of the world by any Tempy," Mrs. Searles said, furiously. "I'll have you know, Benjamin Searles, that I've got life and senses yet, and I'll run my own house my own way 's long as I have."

"Exactly," Miss Tempy said, cheerfully. "That's the way it oughter be. You run it and I'll foller directions. I'm a master hand for follerin' out anything I'm set. You an' I'll gee first-rate. I'm goin' to eat my dinner now, and then we'll talk."

"No, we won't; not a word," returned Mrs. Searles, making a futile attempt to move. Miss Tempy turned her as easily as if she had been a kitten, and stood calmly as a flood of invective was poured out, ending:

"If anybody's mistress here besides me, it's Ruth. I won't have Ruth put upon and set aside. She settles things when I can't."

"All right," Miss Tempy said, "let her settle. I'm agreeable."

Ruth broke into a laugh, and then, shocked at herself, hurried to the bed.

"Go away," her mother said, "go away! Laughing at all I have to suffer. I knew that would be the way."

Ruth would have answered, but Miss Tempy walked out and placed herself at the table.

"Don't you take the head of that table," Mrs. Searles called after her. "I won't have anybody but Ruth in my place."

"I'm agreeable," Miss Tempy answered. "You needn't worry about that."

Ruth, who had hesitated, took the place she had supposed Miss Tempy would claim. Searles looked relieved, and ate his dinner with more gusto than he had shown for weeks. To have an active, sensible woman installed at the helm lifted a burden from all, and a feeling of old times and a suggestion of his youth came over him as he looked at the first face from home he had seen in years. One thing only troubled him; Robert's name might recall the tragedy that had sent Searles West, and as Robert came in to tea that evening he looked anxiously, dreading lest she should make comment. But Miss Tempy had not been in his father's house at the time of Benjamin's leaving, and the name made no impression, though she looked at the boy's face with an interest she seldom felt.

Within a week things had settled into a routine which seemed to have always been theirs. Mrs. Searles protested, scolded, cried, and ended each day with a half-sullen, half-aggressive yielding to the course of events. Her own sense taught her that no such efficient helper could have been in any other way secured, and she even listened with an interest she sought to disguise to the endless stories Miss Tempy had to tell. The daily battle served at least one good purpose. It carried off a certain amount of nervous irritation, and seemed to give her a life hitherto lacking. No tempest could ruffle Miss Tempy's good humor, and the household rejoiced in a new atmosphere. Ruth was still her mother's attendant, but time for much of the old life had come back again. The devil had conquered, as Mr. Brown had feared, and Hannah Searles was a snarling, peevish, malignant invalid, toward whom inevitable pity was often lost in resentment at the almost unbearable provocations of her tongue. Ruth was jarred and fretted a thousand times a day, but Searles, whose own irritability seemed a thing of the past, gave no sign of disgust or annoyance, and met her least wish as promptly as if no weariness or disappointment marred his life.

To Robert she had never again repeated the words which had confounded him, and long ago he had put them away as a sick fancy.

Life had moved on so quietly and uneventfully all this time that it was hard to realize how months were gradually slipping into years. The village itself altered but little. Mr. Brown had left them for two years, but had returned, and the old battles again went on in the office. Mr. Gray had brought a delicate little Eastern wife to the parsonage, and Ruth had found a new outlook for her own life in knowing the gay young girl who had left a city home for the far northern one to which she was even now hardly reconciled. With the new-comer's passionate love of music, which had been cultivated by genuine study, a new world opened to both Robert and Ruth, who till then had heard only the half-bloods' fiddles and the melancholy and abortive little melodeons in the churches. With Mrs. Gray's first summer, and the crowd of gay relatives who flocked northward to "see how Florry bore it," came also the first organ known to the village, small, but exceptionally fine in tone, and seeing the almost reverent wonder and delight with which Robert listened, Mrs. Gray offered to give him all the knowledge she herself possessed. Already he had mastered the melodeon, first picking out tunes by ear and then receiving Ruth's lessons second-hand. Jacky, the small humpback, "big Dawson's" child, whom Robert had taught to read and otherwise befriended, blew the bellows with delight and would have blown it all night willingly. Lockwood remembered that in his college days he had been counted something more than an every-day singer, and even Searles joined his deep bass at intervals to the old tunes they sang on Sunday nights.

Between work and study and this absorbing new occupation Robert had little time for brooding. He had kept his word, and when the dark days came tried to talk away the spell that still possessed him—unavailingly, though. The shadow never wholly lifted. Time was lightening it in part, and at moments Robert seemed to himself free. When the old memory came—sometimes in a dream, or in a chance-word—sending him back into the old, silent brooding, he went out into the deep woods still standing back of the village. Five years had gone since the day he stood before Lockwood and told his story, and in the serious-eyed young engineer there was little trace of the boy as Lockwood had first met him. A man of thirty, all would have said; but he was yet to cast his first vote, looking forward to it with an eagerness born of a genuine faith in the government, not often the portion of "twenty-one" with us. Ruth waited for it, too, with an enthusiasm deep as his own, believing that the addition of such a ballot must work a variety of needed reforms and fully sharing the view she often heard expressed, that Robert was cut out for a judge at least, and would be one some day if people had their rights. To Robert she was still a child, but Lockwood saw something very different; and in the young girl of seventeen, with a sweet, steady face, the steadier and sweeter for the long discipline that had made her patient and silent under her mother's worst outbursts, recognized a woman whose "spirit, still and bright," held promise of rarest happiness for whoever should win and hold it.

If any wonder why he did not enter the lists himself came into people's minds, it soon passed.

Long ago, in spite of occasional phases of sentiment with one and another summer guest, or what were pronounced such, he had been set down by the few marriageable young women of Houghton as "not at all a marrying man." The position had its advantages. He was father-confessor in general to all the young people, only remarking at times that any possibility of his having any feelings himself was quite ignored. But the position satisfied him, and in Robert he seemed to find all that wife or child could have given of interest and devotion.

This for the outside world; but there were other reasons, no cause for the making known of which had ever arisen, and he hoped that life-long silence might shroud them.

CHAPTER XVIII.

AND what of Patty in these years of silence? As one followed another, and Cranstoun at regular intervals appeared, to ask his round of questions, not one word from her indicated that she knew his object. Robert wrote now to Benoni, knowing that she would see the letters, and tempted sometimes to break the silence and address her personally. "Give my love to Mother," he always ended, but in the rare letters that came from Benoni no answering message betrayed that she had the slightest memory of the son who had gone from her. A vow of silence seemed to have sealed her life, but a sense of expectation was always upon her—the expectation that some crime or deadly sin would be the ending of this chronicle of work and study, reaching her punctually at stated intervals and looked for with an eagerness she would never have acknowledged.

As it chanced, Robert had never mentioned Searles's name. She knew he had been always with one family, and thought of them and of Lockwood with a certain gratitude, as having been good to him, but all common feeling had long since been put aside by this imperious possession of one idea. She went through each day's work mechanically and lay down at night to pray, with the intensity of supplication into which all feeling had long ago merged, that God would remove the boy from the world before judgment came.

She had altered little. Her hair could not be whiter, her cheek paler or colder or her dark eyes hold less of human interest, and Cranstoun wrote regularly :

"Yure mar don't look one day older nor younger. She an Benonee is jest the same."

At moments Lockwood wondered why Robert never himself suggested returning, if only for a day. To Robert himself it would have been impossible. The break between the old life and the new seemed sharp and distinct, as if death itself had made the breach. Sometime, far in the future, when life had settled into absolute certainties, he might see them again. In any case he would always know how they fared, and help them when necessary; but, as yet, nothing more. To Patty his non-appearance summed up as part of the perverted tendency whose growth she had watched long before she thought of any decisive action against it, and any occasional longing to at least see his face once more was put away with the sad and bitter memories on which she dwelt now as little as possible. She had sinned and she suffered. If this suffering could in any way avert doom from the boy she would bear it joyfully; but this hope had faded away, and only the hard words sounded day after day in her ears, "The sins of the fathers *shall* be visited upon the children, unto the third and fourth generation."

Robert had come to no settled faith. Deeply religious by nature, the early perversion had been so deep that, in spite of a longing, at times filling him with almost anguish, faith and peace seemed impossible gifts. Argue as he would, the old belief still held him in chains, and only at rare moments, as the flood of rich sound poured from the church organ under his fingers and he looked up to feel the sunshine from the chancel window lying on his face, did he lose himself, and rise into an atmosphere serene and triumphant, to which no jarring thought—no hard memory—could penetrate.

The ministers had long since ceased to urge him into their folds, and Mr. Brown was disposed at times . to regard his life of almost ascetic morality as more of a snare than the pronounced sinfulness or decided worldliness of most other young men. Mr. Brown, however, had a variety of thoughts just at present seriously damaging to any work at proselyting, and it was a singular fact that among the reputable elders and discreet mothers in Israel in his congregation, there was not one from whom he did not shrink as he thought of confiding to them the possibilities in his mind.

In these years, since his first coming to Houghton, his wife had died and his three boys scattered to various quarters, one of them being then in the State University and bidding fair to make an unusual student. Hard-working, silent and patient, this wife of his youth, chosen among the class to which he then belonged, had been cherished to the last; but in the three years since her death a new ambition had sprung up. Still in his prime, a man to whom all the country looked up, and whose keen humor and strong common sense gave him a power with the rough population of the region gaining steadily every year, he reached out for something more than life had ever given him, and in his deepest heart called Ruth Searles his own. That Ruth herself could object—the child whom he had loved and whom his wife had petted, mourning always that only boys had come to them—he would not believe. That she was sought after, he knew. His own oldest boy had long ago affirmed that when rich enough he was coming back for Ruth, but Ruth only smiled; a sweet, but somewhat cold smile, which held the property of quenching unnecessary or displeasing ardor while yet giving no reasonable ground of offense.

One day Mr. Brown had spoken, and to his own mortification and distress, and apparently quite as much to Ruth's, had met a decided, unequivocal refusal. That this man, who seemed to her older than her father, could be in earnest she would not believe; but, as he saw her angry incredulity, and drawing nearer tried, with all the fond words which came to him suddenly, to tell her what he hoped for, she burst into tears.

"What have I done?" she sobbed. "What can I have done to make you think of such a dreadful thing?"

"Is it so dreadful?" said the minister tenderly. "I am a great deal older, but you are older than your years, Ruth, and you will find I have a young heart."

"Don't; oh, don't!" said Ruth, putting out her hands. "I didn't know you thought of me when you kept coming. I thought it was Miss Tempy."

"What!" Mr. Brown said fiercely. Then, struck by the incongruity of this vision with the one he had been silently cherishing, burst into a laugh, which startled Ruth as thoroughly as his words had done.

"Please go away," she said apprehensively, not sure but that he had taken leave of his senses altogether.

"Not till you tell me you will think about it," he answered, recovering himself. "There is nothing so dreadful, if you will only think."

Ruth shrunk still more.

"It is impossible," she said decisively. "You must never say such things again. Please go."

"Then there is someone else," the minister answered slowly. "I thought that might be. If that is so, and he is worthy, I can consent to be still. Is there?"

Ruth colored painfully.

"You have no right to ask," she said.

"But I have. Loving you as I do gives the right. If there is, and I know it, I stand aside. If there is not, I shall not give up hope. Tell me, Ruth."

"No," she said at last nervously. "No one has spoken."

"Do you *love* any one?"

"You are very hard," Ruth said indignantly, "for you know I must tell the truth. I do. Now go."

The minister's ruddy face grew pale for a moment.

"That ends it," he said slowly. "God bless him, and God bless you, my little Ruth."

"Oh, forgive me!" Ruth said, with a sudden relenting as he took her hands. "I didn't know—he doesn't know—you must never tell," and with a fresh burst of tears she hurried away. Miss Tempy, who met her as she ran up-stairs, looked sharply at the minister, who had lingered long enough to put down all traces of agitation, and stood quietly by the table as she came in.

"What's upset the child?" she said. "Ruth doesn't cry for nothing. She hasn't done it ten times in the five years I've been here."

"A little trouble she was telling me," the minister said, smiling involuntary at Miss Tempy's fierce manner, as of a venerable and excitable old hen with one chicken. "Nothing that won't settle itself. We old folks meddle too much."

"Hm!" Miss Tempy said; and, under cover of this comprehensive ejaculation, he passed out and up the village street. His heart was very sore; he wanted human comfort; and as he walked rapidly on till the turn to the Point was reached and he saw Robert going slowly down the narrow path, he hailed him. Robert turned and waited, noting the minister's troubled face, and wondering what had altered its usual brisk cheerfulness. The two walked on together, talking of whatever came uppermost, and as they turned, the elder man laid his hand on Robert's for a moment, as if to draw from its warm young strength.

"You are not well, I am sure," Robert said.

"Yes, I am; well enough. But "—the impulse had come, and he yielded to it—"I'm a fool. I've offered myself to Ruth, and she won't have me. Why I'm telling you I don't know. Because I am a fool, I reckon."

Robert was silent. The shock of surprise was too intense to admit of words.

"I see you agree with me," Mr. Brown said, a little bitterly. "You think a fool's presumption deserves a fool's punishment. Well, I've got it."

Still Robert was silent, till, seeing the color mounting to his old friend's face, he spoke:

"I'm very glad. I mean I am very sorry. I did not know you thought of such a thing. Poor Ruth!"

"Poor Ruth!" Mr. Brown repeated, testily. "Not at all. Poor me! Ruth can have her pick of all the young fellows in town. I wish I was one of them. God forgive me!—a swearing, rowdy set, the most of them. I'd better go home and settle my mind."

Mr. Brown hurried off, and Robert, turning again, went on to the spot where he and Lockwood so often sat, and threw himself upon the mat of pine needles

covering the ground. What a blind idiot he had been!
Ruth, little Ruth, who had been the sweetest thing
he had ever known, and who seemed till that moment
still a child, was a child no longer. They had been
brother and sister, but the few words still sounding in
his ears had ended that tie. What she might feel
he could not tell; but in his own soul Robert knew
that the love he had felt in these years of life together
had suddenly shown its real face, and ended such life
forever.

"She is mine," he said, passionately. "How dared
that man speak to her!"

Then, as he started up, he sank back again and his
face grew deadly pale.

"What right have I to burden her life with mine?"
he said, softly. "She knows nothing, and how can I
tell her; or if I tell her, what use? 'Cursed with a
curse.' How do I dare think of tangling up another
life in mine? and yet—Oh, my God!—how can I do
without it?"

He hid his face, and lay there silently till the stars
came out, and the night wind brought with it "mur-
murs and scents of the infinite sea" over whose track-
less depths the struggling soul voyaged, seeking the
safe harbor, nearer than he knew. All the years rose
before him, and he set his teeth fiercely as he remembered what renunciation lay at the heart of each: what
force of repression, what sense that God himself had
outlawed him.

"Father! Father!" he cried, whether to the human father he had never known or the divine, all-loving one, he could not tell; but, as he cried, a strange quiet fell upon him. Doubt, miserable questioning, sharp protest against fate, died away. There must and should be something in the world for him. He would have faith. He would seek the happiness he had not dared to dream could be his, and if it came would take it as a final answer to all doubt. God was and would be good to a soul that longed for truth, but longed, too, for rest and peace and love. He bared his head and stood under the stars, and, like Jacob of old, vowed that if this desire of his heart were granted the Lord should be his God forevermore; then, with bowed head but with the same strange quiet filling him, went home in the darkness and slept, dreamlessly and deep.

CHAPTER XIX.

IN those hours of life in which years are lived, and we wake to a new day with the consciousness that between us and yesterday is a great gulf which no man can pass, it is hard to believe that no physical change has set its seal upon the mental. We meet our own eyes in the glass with the strange look that comes with seeking recognition there, and wonder that the face bears no outward token of the work that brain and soul have wrought. We guard ourselves jealously lest some tell-tale glance or new expression reveal the secret. Yet there is no need. No change is there. No friend, save from our own word, will ever know what the day has brought. Youth does not believe this, but middle-life knows it, and, thanks to the fog of selfishness or absorption in which each soul is most often wrapped, we may meet a hundred times a day and neither give nor receive token that a great sorrow or a great joy has been the portion of any one among us. Better so; for to each one comes, sooner or later, the knowledge that even the tenderest human love is of little avail when the soul is learning its lessons, and that, lean as we may, at last we walk through the valley alone. Alone there, and alone in the mysterious way beyond—unless the soul know, as souls can, "I am not alone, for the Father is with me."

To Robert, with whom another crisis had come, it seemed as if everyone must read his old pain and new hope in his face, and he held himself with even more than usual quietness as he entered the dining-room. Ruth was not there, and a thrill of disappointment went through him. He had wanted to look at her in the light of this new knowledge and carry the picture of the gray eyes and the sweet, steady face, as he felt it must soon meet his look. But in a moment he was glad. What new meanings were to be found should not come under others' eyes. He would take her on the lake that afternoon, or to their old haunt on the Point, and tell her there all he longed to pour out. It seemed now as if they had never spoken. All old knowledge was useless till fused in this new fire, of longing for an understanding and for the words he hardly doubted that Ruth would speak. Their lives must be one. It was not within possibility that any other human being could claim his right. He could hardly wait, yet the day's work must be done, and he listened eagerly as Miss Tempy answered Searles's question,

"Where's Ruth?"

"Mis' Gray's help came down early to get her. The

baby's sick, and Ruth thought maybe she shouldn't get back before tea-time."

"She might 'a' said so, then," snapped the invalid, whose bed was drawn opposite the door in order that if so inclined she could join in the conversation. "She only said she was going up awhile; 'tendin' to everybody but her own!"

Miss Tempy sniffed dangerously, but was silent. The one point on which she could be roused was Ruth, and the endless exactions made upon her by the invalid, whose last remnant of self-control had fled long ago, and who alternated between a slow fret—as wearing as the ancient "continual dropping," and vicious bursts of temper—exhausting everyone but herself.

"Last!" Mr. Brown had been heard to say in an unguarded moment, in answer to the wonder from one of his church people, "how long that poor, suffering skeleton of a woman was likely to last." "Last! She'll outlast you or me, any day. She's pickled in sin, and tongue and temper are about all there is left of her. Part of it's her condition, but I've seen folks as badly off look as if they were on the very threshold of heaven. Satan's got such a tight grip of her here he's in no hurry to begin operations in the next world. I do suppose nobody but the doctor ever knows just how much misery a bad-tempered invalid can sow round, and sometimes I feel like gagging her an hour a day, just to give the family a little peace. It's beyond belief, the way her tongue can go on."

This morning a slight scorch in Miss Tempy's generally faultless toast had stirred up even more than the
usual commotion in the sick room, which Ruth's
absence seemed to intensify. Robert, who had
gone in for a moment to lift the invalid, sat down
and almost unconsciously fixed his eyes full upon
her, noting the hard lines, the multitude of fine
wrinkles, the pinched nose and lips, and the cold
blue eyes as curiously as if they belonged to some
unknown specimen. How could Ruth bear it, hour
after hour—day after day? Was it her duty to bear
it? And why should not justice speak here, and
order into silence the unreasoning outrage of this
pestilent, snarling tongue? What gleam of dislike or
resolution may have been visible in his eyes he did not
know, but Mrs. Searles suddenly grew silent and looked at him fixedly.

"The truest thing you've done since you came into
this house," she said, in a low tone. "I knew the
devil was there, but you never showed him so plain before. You think you'll have your way; but I'll beat
you yet, for all your cunning."

Robert was silent, silence having become the family
rule under the countless complaints and accusations
poured out day after day.

"You and your father think you humbug me with
your quiet ways," she went on, with concentrated bitterness. "You'll find you never can. Did you suppose I haven't known for years who you are and what

you want? The property's mine, and you shall never get it."

"You have said this before," Robert said, after a look which showed him this was no fancy or raving. "What do you mean?"

"I mean that you are Benjamin Searles's son, by that vile woman that sent you here, and that you and he are joined together to cheat me. You never have. I hated you for it, and I hate you now."

"It is wasted hate," Robert answered, quietly, as the first amazement passed away. "You have deceived yourself uselessly. I am the son of a man who died twenty years ago, and my mother is a sorrowful woman whose name you have no right to take upon your lips. Let this be the last time you dare use it so," he added, an intensity of passionate resentment suddenly leaping through his veins.

His eyes flashed. He rose and stood over her. Mrs. Searles cowered as though under a coming blow. For a moment he held her in that look, then passed out, and went to his work, astonishment at such hallucination still filling him. The day went in a half dream. Thoughts of the future blended curiously with memories brought up by the wild words of the angry woman, and with wonder how this might affect his hopes.

Work ended, he went hastily home, hoping to find Ruth and end all uncertainties.

"She ain't here," Miss Tempy said, as he put his

head into the dining-room. "The baby's worse, and she's going to stay all night."

Robert went up to his room, and sitting down by the table took up a book. But he could not read, and when Searles presently passed the door called him in. Dwight had not returned, and the necessity for some companionship was strong upon him. Searles looked at him intently, wondering what could have brought about such disturbance.

"You haven't had any bad news?" he asked, presently, in a pause in their talk over a new process of extracting ore from the rock.

"No!" Robert said, hastily, and then, following an impulse more suddenly than was his wont, "No; not at all. But I am thinking of something that must be settled at once, and part of the work lies in your hands."

Searles moved uneasily, and the change in his countenance Robert interpreted as understanding of his purpose and disapproval of its expression.

"You know what I want, I see," he said. "I hoped you would take it differently. You can't wonder at my loving Ruth, or that I want her for my wife if she will consent."

Searles rose suddenly, and took both of Robert's hands.

"It's been the one desire of my heart," he said. "There's no other man alive I'd be willing to give her to."

"Wait," Robert said, puzzled at the sudden change, but bent, now that he had spoken, upon having no concealments between them. "You know nothing of me, but you must know everything. Perhaps when you do you will be less willing. Sit down. It is a long story."

Searles made a movement as if to check it; then sat down, and listened silently with averted head as the long-buried memories came to light once more. A struggle was going on in his own mind. Should he still keep silent, and not mar the new hope by any possible harm from his own words, or should he meet honesty with honesty, and at last stand free from this life-long burden? He was silent; Robert as he ended looked eagerly at him and was startled at the paleness of his face.

"It's my turn now," Searles said hastily, as if dreading his own weakness and determined to lose no more time. "You needn't have told me a word. Before you were born I knew it all, and more; and I'll tell you how it came, and what it did to me. I'm the man whose testimony hung your father. I'm the man your mother cursed for leading him away. And I've carried a heavy heart from that day to this. When you came here, a little boy, and I heard your name and looked at your face, I prayed that I might have a chance to help you, and when you came here again, five years ago, I took you in as if you were my own. You know that well. I've wanted to tell you, but I never dared. I thought how it might be between you and Ruth, and I said that if I gave the dearest thing I had it would atone for the harm I did the father. Robert, I never meant to do him any harm. I loved him more than men do love one another. He was dearer than a brother. He forgave me at the last, but I never forgave myself; and now that I tell you that you may have Ruth, I ask Robert Saunders's son to forgive me too."

Searles had spoken with bent head. He looked up now to meet eyes fixed on him in so horror-stricken a gaze that he sprang up.

"Good God!" he said. "Are you going mad, Robert? What is the matter?"

"Don't touch me," the young man said, shaking off his hands and rising slowly and painfully. The two men faced one another—the elder anxious and alarmed, the younger with set teeth and a look of deepening passion he sought to master.

"You—liar!" he said, at last, slowly, between his teeth. "You—living a lie day by day—cheating me into a life I would have run from as I would have run from pestilence! How dare you do this thing? Am I to call you father? The man who brought my own father to his grave and sneaked away, to cheat the son when the time came and kill his soul as he had helped to kill the father? By God! I could strike you down as you stand there!"

Robert raised his clenched fist, but as he raised it

Lockwood, who had come into the room unheard, sprang forward and caught him.

" Are you both beside yourselves?" he said. " What do you mean?"

Robert looked at him a moment, still struggling. The veins in his forehead were swollen—his whole face desperate and wild. Then his arm relaxed and fell at his side. A look of despair took the place of the fierce rage that had moved him. He caught his hat from the table and in a moment was gone.

" Go after him," Searles said, hoarsely. " He'll do himself a mischief."

" Tell me first what you have been about," Lockwood answered. " I must know what I am doing before I speak."

" If you know his story, as you've always said," Searles replied, " you don't need much telling. He wanted to marry Ruth and told me himself, and I've just told him I'm the man that went shares in every scrape with his father, and at last sent him to his death. It's a fine mess. See if your words will straighten it."

" Poor fellow !" Lockwood said, but the tone and look brought a sudden change in Searles.

" Go quick," he said, " and try and bring him back. I wish Ruth was home."

Lockwood hurried out, stopped by Miss Tempy, whose tea-bell had rung long before unheeded:

" Is there anything I can do?" she said quietly, but

with a scared face. "I know something dreadful has happened."

"Keep Mrs. Searles from suspecting anything," Lockwood answered, "and don't let Ruth know. That is all."

"It's too late for the first," Miss Tempy said. "These scantling houses let noise through them like so much paper, and she heard 'em. Their voices rose like the wind."

"Then try and keep her quiet," Lockwood answered, breaking away, and Miss Tempy, shaking her head, returned to the room where Mrs. Searles lay chuckling, as if well satisfied with the storm.

"I saw the devil in him," she said. "He's begun to show all round. Ben! Ben! I want you. It's about time we had a square talk. Come here."

Searles had entered the dining-room and now answered her summons mechanically; but as she broke out into the same charges made long ago and repeated to-day to Robert, he stepped forward and took her arms as though he would have shaken her.

"You fool!" he said. "So that is what has ailed you. Now hush it, once for all. It is a lie and you know it; and now you shall know all there is to hear, and then be silent. If I ever hear word of it again, to him or to me, you've looked your last at me in this world."

Miss Tempy stood near, aghast at the outburst and

more aghast as the story ended, and Hannah Searles, sobbing with terror, lay silent, not daring to answer.

"The Lord help us all!" said Miss Tempy. "It's out of our hands now, and may He settle it in the best way."

"There's no settling such doings," Searles said with a groan. "They manage themselves, and there's no help now for any of us. God help poor Ruth when she knows."

"Keep it from her, if there's a grain sense left among you," said Miss Tempy angrily. "Because a tornado's gone through the house there's no reason it should take her head off too. Poor lamb! She has trouble enough every day. I vow and declare I'll take her and put for home if this goes a word further."

"It all depends on Robert," said Searles, heavily. "He's had a hard time amongst us, but if he will hear reason and settle down she never need know."

"I don't know," Miss Tempy answered, drearily. "I don't know as it can be so. We've just got to wait. It's the worst snarl I've seen yet, but it can be untwisted, and maybe 't will. I don't know."

CHAPTER XX.

IGHT had settled down before Lockwood found Robert. The crisp September air grew keener as the sun set, and a pale aurora flickered in the north—first signal of coming winter. First, to the Point, where so many phases of life and thought had been talked out, and then, failing to find him there, on to the old wood-road and a clearing where a trapper's deserted cabin stood, and where Robert sometimes went in search of absolute solitude;—no sign of his presence, and Lockwood grew more and more anxious. The wind was rising and the lake rough. If he had gone out in his canoe he was in danger of being swamped. Lockwood hurried back to the dock, but as he passed the works it suddenly occurred to him that Robert might have come here, as the most unlikely place in which search would be made. He opened the door with his own pass-key and entered the office. The moon shone faintly through the grimy window, and sitting near it he could just discern the outline of a dark figure.

He drew a chair near it and sat down in silence, weary with his long run, but too full of pity for any thought of self. He laid his hand on Robert's. For a moment it was pushed aside, then caught and held with the grip of a drowning man. Presently Robert lifted his head, and in the faint light Robert saw his face was ghastly.

"I must go away, Dwight," he said. "The steamer passes here at midnight. I must go then."

"Where, my poor boy?"

"Home. I mean, to where my mother and father used to be. I have been thinking what to do. I can never see Ruth again, but I must know now *exactly* all that happened. I have plenty of money—I saved a good deal, you know—and I can stay long enough to find out everything for myself. Then I will go somewhere and work again till I die. I did think of killing myself to-night. I had the pistol in my hand. There it is on the table. Then I thought all I had ever heard was hearsay. Mother and Searles tell the same story, but I want to see and hear for myself. There's an old uncle of hers at Lowgate who was with her, and who can tell the whole, and there are court records, I suppose."

Robert spoke in a dull, heavy voice. His hands had fallen again.

"Do one thing for me," he said. "I can't go back to the house. Go up now and pack a valise of what I must take with me. When I am gone, pack everything else and store it here, and when I know what to do you can send it to me."

"Robert, it mustn't end so," Lockwood said. "Try and think farther than your own pain. Do you want to kill Ruth?"

"Ruth knows nothing—thank God. God!" he repeated with a bitter mockery. "Let it go. Thank *Something*, I have never spoken to her, and she will not know."

"What will your going mean to her?"

"A freak—anything that is outrageous and in harmony with my life and fate. Her mother has a belief that may account for it."

"You have no right to make the innocent suffer," Lockwood said. "Robert, you shall not go till you have had more time to think."

"If I could tear out the power of thought, and end this thing once for all, I would do it," he answered bitterly. "Dwight, last night at this time I believed in God. I had actually worked myself into that state where I believed he meant me to have some happiness. I saw long, quiet years with the woman I loved stretching before me. I prayed. I have read prayers in a church; but last night I prayed from my own soul, for the first time in my life, and thought I had an answer then and there. I was quite at rest. The curse seemed hidden by his love. I believed it might pass. To-night I sit here with every hope a lie, and God's love the worst lie of all. I have wanted to murder; first that man, then myself. The sins of the fathers have descended. I am a murderer, too. Cursed with a curse! Let go, Dwight! After to-night I will touch no human hand."

Lockwood was silent. No word could meet this intolerable pain, but an anguish of pity filled him. He held the cold hands and prayed silently for help.

"Robert," he said at last, "only wait a day. You are beside yourself with sorrow. Wait, and you will see there is a way out. It is horrible darkness, but God is here. He will lead you. You are not left. He cannot leave a soul in such torment. Wait."

"What do you know of it?" said Robert fiercely. "You have never felt the burden of hereditary sin. You have never struggled to believe, and found your best effort tossed aside and your soul bound down in a chain forged before you were born. Talk of what you understand, but leave this thing alone."

Lockwood drew a long, shuddering breath.

"Listen to me," he said. "You ask what I know of your pain or struggle—what knowledge of mine can take in the sense of bondage that you feel. I wish I had told you before; but I will tell you now. The chain that limits you is a gossamer thread compared to the one that binds me body and soul; yet I believe in God. My own hand would have taken my life long ago if I had not believed."

"What do you mean?" Robert said. Something in

Lockwood's tone roused him to a consciousness outside himself.

"You have heard me talk of my mother," Lockwood said slowly, and as if each word came with pain. "I remember my father as he was when I was a very little fellow, and then he disappeared. We went to a distant town. My mother wore widow's weeds all her life, and till my second year in college I supposed him dead. My younger brother—a beautiful boy, and making ready to enter the same college—suddenly developed symptoms of insanity. He was placed in an asylum; and before many months I knew that he was a raving maniac. It broke my mother's heart. She had always been frail, and now she simply faded away. But before she died she told me—" Lockwood's voice broke. He struggled to command himself; then went on:

"My father was living, but hopelessly insane. For eighteen years he had been in an insane asylum, sometimes raving, sometimes passive and silent, but a hopeless case. His father had died in an asylum. His grandfather had committed suicide in a sudden attack. Far back as one could follow the family thread, one or more in each generation had ended their days under this cloud. My mother had read and thought deeply, and as she lay there dying she said to me: 'Dwight, I sinned against you unknowingly, but I sinned in bringing you into the world at all. I was very young, and your father and I loved one another very

deeply, and though I knew the family taint I had
no thought of what it meant. We had no right to
marry—no right to bring children into the world to an
inheritance of misery. What I suffer now is a just
punishment for my sin, though it was the sin of ignorance, and I must suffer, it seems to me, even in the
next world in knowing to what I have doomed you.
If you want me to die in such peace as I can, you must
promise me that never—never, no matter how tempted
—will you marry, or give life to a child who may curse
you for the gift. Promise me now.'

" I hesitated. It seemed as if a black wall suddenly
shut me in. I was not in love, but I had an ardent
nature—a man's hopes. I had looked forward to my
own home. I wanted love, and all that love means.

"My mother's eyes held me. It was as if her soul
forced me to speech.

"'My darling,' she said, 'it is horrible. I cannot
bear it, but I must insist. There is no safety unless
you promise. Since Arnold left me, and I have thought
of the years before him, and that beautiful soul cut off
from all hope, I have prayed that he might die. I have
agonized over you both. You are like my father,
Dwight, and there is no taint there, but we cannot tell.
You have the other blood, too, and you can never feel
sure. You must promise.'

" She broke into tears that were terrible. She was
dying then, and dying in this struggle for me. I took
her into my arms. 'Be easy, Mother,' I said. 'As

God sees us, no child of mine shall ever live to share such knowledge.'

"She had no words left. She held me fast till I felt her hold loosen, and laid her down. She looked up one moment. 'Forgive me, Dwight,' she said, and was gone.

"Robert, there was a year in which I raged against my fate, and called God to account for allowing me to live at all. And then I learned, hard as it was, to believe what I have told you, that heredity is not God's *curse* but God's *school* for his world. Through ignorance life had come to me. Through knowledge I must submit to the hard conditions—renounce the hopes that should have been mine by right, and find in others' lives the life denied me. Out of all that blackness of darkness at last came light and hope. My 'little gleam of time between two eternities' should not be spoiled by a wail over its deprivations. There was still a world of endeavor before me—of enjoyment, of acquirement. God's peace was with me as I settled at last into the faith I hold. He pities me. He loves me. His strength leads me through every dark hour, and they are more than you have ever known. The life I wanted is taken from me, but I shall have it, or something that will fill its place, in the eternity to come. Robert, is it true that your struggle is a riddle to me?"

"God help you," Robert said low.

"He does, and he will help you. I have told you what I never expected to tell any human being, Robert.

Now I want you to promise me one thing. Go now, for I believe it best for you, but come back when you have found out all you want to know. Whatever may be decided after that, come back. No such taint mars your life as mars mine. Away from here you can think it all out. Will you come back? Not to stay, necessarily, but to settle your plan of life definitely?"

"I will come," Robert said; "but you don't know what you ask, Dwight."

"I do know, and that is why I ask. Now I am going for your valise, Robert, unless you will come yourself. No? Well, then—but first"——

Dwight kneeled by the table, still holding Robert's hand, and in a few solemn words—the first words of prayer the young man had ever heard from him—commended him, soul and body, to the God who through dark ways would lead him into light. "Thy love is eternal," he said. "It never fails us. Only we fail to take hold of it and make it ours. Lead him day and night till out of his sorrow he passes into thy peace. Give him his heart's desire if it is thy will. Let him know, that underneath are thy everlasting arms, and once more bring us to one another, or make him know that, together or apart, we seek the same country; that thou hast prepared some better thing for him."

Once more, as in the boy's first great sorrow, Dwight, as he rose, bent and kissed him, then went silently away.

An hour later the great steamer touched at the

pier, and, with one long pressure of his friend's hand, Robert went on board, and stood watching the moonlit town till it was lost in the distance; pacing the deck till chilled with the cold of early morning, and then, worn with feeling, went to his state-room and lost himself in sleep.

CHAPTER XXI.

UTH walked swiftly down the village street in the chill morning air. The sun had risen and the fog was lifting, and as she looked off, trying to penetrate the mist, it broke suddenly, and the white sails of a schooner were seen making for the landing. Weary with her long watch, and yearning—with a desire she would hardly admit to herself—for an end to uncertainty in the words she felt sure must soon be spoken, she stood for a moment watching the slow roll of the vessel as it tacked, listening to the beat of the long waves on the shore, and trying to make to-day seem part of all the days that had gone before. In the hours just passed, in which she had sat by the sleeping baby, all her childhood seemed to have been buried. Her cheeks still burned as she recalled the minister's persistent question, and the strange thrill that had gone through her as a veil seemed to lift and show her for what love she did care, and what name came almost to her lips as the only one she could ever know as that of lover or husband.

"Robert doesn't know; Robert may never care," she told herself over and over; and over and over came the answer: "He will know; he has always cared." In spite of doubt and weariness, even shame that her love was given before any asking, her heart was light. She could wait—wait for years if need be—for youth and life and love were her portion. Her eyes filled with tears of deep, quiet feeling as she looked once more toward the schooner, now sailing straight on to harbor, and her lips murmured, "And so He bringeth them unto the haven where they would be."

"Big Dennison," as he passed her, pulled off his cap and looked after her.

"There's a look of the Howly Mother herself on her face," he muttered, "an' she a Protestant. May all the saints lead her into the true Church!"

Arrived at home, Ruth ran up the steps and into her mother's room.

"Baby is better," she said. "I've been away longer than I meant, Mother, but I knew you would spare me."

"It don't make any matter," Mrs. Searles said, feebly. Ruth came nearer and looked at her. Something in her face had come or gone. Ruth could not tell which. The expression of settled evil-temper had given way to pain. The hard lines were all there, but also a sorrowful look the girl had never seen, and she spoke in quick alarm,

"You are not worse, Mother? I wish I had not left you."

" No, I'm no worse," Mrs. Searles answered, and lay silent. Ruth went to Miss Tempy, who put on a jaunty air which could not disguise the fact that her eyes were red and her cheeks pale.

"Something is wrong," Ruth said. "What is it?"

"Fiddle-de-dee, child!" Miss Tempy said. "What should be wrong? Go and lie down till breakfast. You've been up all night. How's the baby?"

"Better," Ruth answered, with her eyes fixed on Miss Tempy so intently that she turned away irritably.

"What's the use of making your eyes into gimlets, and screwing in that way, Ruth? I wish you'd set the table for me."

Ruth turned away silently and went into the dining-room, looking every moment for Robert's appearance and an explanation of the strange feeling in the house. Lockwood came down as the bell rang, and her father followed, pale and haggard, with a vain attempt to carry himself as usual. "Where is Robert?" she asked, at last, hearing no sound overhead.

"Didn't you tell her?" Searles said, looking reproachfully at Miss Tempy. "He's had to go away last night, Ruth—on—business."

"He is coming back," Lockwood said, quickly, noting the girl's deadly paleness and quick bracing as if to meet some blow. "He had to go, but he is coming back again."

"Didn't he leave any word for me?" Ruth said, try-

ing to collect herself but trembling with a dread she
could not put down.

"No," Lockwood said, slowly, doubting what words
were best, and wishing she had been told less suddenly.
"He had some news that troubled him and went at
midnight."

"His mother," Ruth said, relieved. "If she is sick,
of course he had to go just so hurriedly. She is not
dead? Poor Robert!"

"No, she is not dead," Lockwood said.

"Who brought the news? Some runner? Letters
never come in any way but that. I don't even know
how a letter could go to her by post. He is coming
home again soon; or will he wait till it is all
over?"

"I'll tell you all about it after breakfast, Ruth,"
Searles said, feeling as if his voice sounded from some
space beyond him and would startle the girl, who now
made a pretense of eating but watched for her father's
first movement from the table. It came at last, and
Ruth followed him wonderingly as he turned away
from the usual sitting-room and went up to Robert's.
Miss Tempy heard the key turn in the door as they
entered, and she sat down and cried silently.

"I'm a fool," she said, presently, wiping away her
tears with vigor. "Out of your doleful dumps, Tempy
Perkins, and keep your spirits up for the sake of sense
and reason! What's done is done, an' cryin' ain't
goin' to help it; but I'd give one o' my fingers to put

things where they were a week ago. I feel as if a funeral was goin' on."

"It is a funeral," Lockwood said, softly. "The young girl who went into that room can never come out again; yet I am not sure but that the woman we shall see will be finer and better. I believe a truer life is waiting for everyone who has shared this sadness and pain."

Lockwood's own eyes were heavy and his face worn with sorrow, but he smiled with all his old cheer as he left the room.

"One of the Lord's anointed, if ever a human being was!" Miss Tempy ejaculated, and added: "And to think I should ever say that of that good-for-nothing Dwight!"

Lockwood was right. To Ruth, who listened at first with utter incredulity, then with shocked acceptance, and at last under the sense that all hope was crushed, it had been as a passing through the grave and gate of death. Pity for her father for a time overmastered all other feeling, but as he turned at last and looked at her, as if his words had placed a gulf between them that no power could span, she sprang to him, and held him as if her slight arms were a shield between him and all the world.

"Poor Father! darling Father!" she murmured. "Did you think I should hate you? I love you a million times more! We haven't anybody but one another now. Oh, why didn't you tell me before!"

"I couldn't," Searles said, cut to the heart at what the reproach in the tone implied. "I couldn't bear to lose you, child, and I thought you would turn against me and despise me."

Ruth's only answer was another close embrace; but when he had left her and gone to the day's work she bowed her head on Robert's table and sat there in silence. Life and youth and love were hers still; but where was the glow of faith and hope she had known only two hours ago? Every tie in the past had been swept away by this new knowledge. If Robert came back, how could he look at her save with loathing? Guiltless as her father was, he must forever be felt as one link in the fatal chain that had brought the elder Robert to a wretched death, and his sin was visited upon her. How could she bear it? Ruth wrung her hands as the sharp anguish rolled over her like a flood; then covered her eyes as if to shut out the long vista of desolate years that suddenly opened before her, gray and barren, with one narrow path in which her feet must walk. Lost in pain she sat till a knock sounded at the door, and she rose, trying to steady herself.

"It's me, Ruth," Miss Tempy's voice said. "You needn't open till you want to. Your mother's calling for you."

Ruth pushed back her heavy hair and collected every force.

"I am coming," she said quietly, and then fell on

her knees. When she rose her face wore its usual look of sweet, steady gravity.

"I can still love him," she said, half aloud. " I can not do anything but love him. It may help him."

One more look about the room. A watch-guard that Robert had worn lay on the table, and she took it up, pressed it to her lips, then put it about her neck and under her dress so that it could not be detected, and went down to her mother.

She expected fretfulness, but none came. The shock of knowing what trouble had been wrought seemed to have silenced Hannah Searles, and in that silence the past had come up vividly. She remembered Searles's gay face and hearty laugh and the strange change a little time had wrought, wishing now, too late, that she had understood then, and perhaps have had a different life for both. Indignation that he had deceived her rose at times, and then the feeling that too much importance had been given to it from the beginning, and that Robert had no right to resent as he did the wrong of which Searles was guiltless in intention. And curiously, too, came the sense of disgrace, that the man whose name she bore had been mixed up with a murder trial.

She, Hannah Bowen, whose people had all been respectable church members, avoiding scandals and obeying all neighborhood laws with scrupulous exactness, to be the wife of a man who had smuggled, and raced horses, and at last helped to condemn his best friend to death! And in this resentment the fleeting wish that things might have been different was lost, and when Ruth went in she lay in the old silence which had marked her first knowledge of her fate; a silence become now her habit.

With the change she weakened physically. Dr. Barnet shook his head when finally called in.

"There's an unaccountable difference," he said to Miss Tempy. "I thought she was good for years. You need not be surprised, now, to see her life flicker out at any moment like a candle."

Shocked and sympathetic, Miss Tempy kept vigilant watch; but the end came sooner than even the doctor dreamed, and as Searles one morning drew up the curtain and turned to look, the thin face was set and still, and Hannah Searles's troubled spirit had passed to such rest as it could know.

There could be no mourning like that which follows the passing of one who has loved as well as lived among us, yet her death left a blank that needed long time to fill. The peevish voice seemed yet to call to Ruth, and the girl sprang up at times to answer it, with the feeling that her long work in the little room could not be over, and even the wish that the weary ministering might still go on.

October had nearly ended and only one letter had come from Robert; a mere note written at Detroit just after reaching there, and saying that he should probably remain a few days. It was generally understood in the village that his mother's dangerous illness had called him away, and Lockwood allowed the impression to remain. Searles, as manager of the works, held his place for him, filling it temporarily with one of the boys who had grown up in the Company's service, but in his own mind he had small thought that Robert would ever return. Lockwood cared for Ruth with a tenderness that often brought tears to her eyes, and in all ways the old life remained the old life as far as possible. Work and study went on, and he planned so that small time for brooding should be possible, talking of Robert's return as if it might be at any hour, and never admitting the thought of any changed relation. Ruth never made answer. The shadow hung too darkly over any future to allow one gleam of light, and Lockwood could only judge her hopelessness by the deeper quietness—the entire passivity—with which she followed out any suggestion. So the month passed. The first gray November days were upon them, and soon the long winter would shut them in and chain the great lake in its six months' fetters.

CHAPTER XXII.

ROBERT did not leave his cabin till late the next afternoon, and the steward looked with undisguised curiosity at the young man who had slept through all the noise of repeated landings, as well as disregarded the claims of the meals, which to other passengers were an unfailing duty and resource.

Sleep had soon left him. The long hours after waking had passed first in an almost stupor; only the sharp pain of remembrance darting athwart it and rousing him to a passionate sense of wrong, fast becoming a reckless defiance.

As the supper-bell sounded he entered the cabin, ate all he could force himself to take, and then went up to the upper deck, from which the lights along the river front of the city could now clearly be seen. There was a life, in which he could lose himself. There was work, if work were wanted; but suppose, now, that he tried play instead? He had lived as if pleasure were only a name, yet here, almost at hand, waited all that could fill days and hours with delight. This hard past

—a past he had fought against till its last crushing blow had laid him in the dust—why should he battle with it longer? If the curse must work, then let every passion have its way. See what virtue lay in wine—in anything that young men had told him meant pleasure. He recalled the face of a summer guest in the last year—a young lawyer, who had studied him with unconcealed curiosity, and, as he said good-by, had added: "When you get ready for a little knowledge of *real* life, Saunders, come to me, and I'll put you through." He looked at the address in his note-book. The eager desire to hasten on to New England was gone. Only new pain lay in its fulfillment, and from more pain he shrank. A map of the city which they were approaching hung in the cabin. He went in and studied it intently, finding the avenue where young Mitchell lived, and resolving to go to him at once. Whatever it might seem well to do afterward, at least sorrow should be buried now in ways that men of the world did bury sorrow. If these proved fruitless, it was time enough then to settle on future action.

He took a room in a quiet hotel in a side street, and after a restless and disturbed night went early to the office of his summer acquaintance, who greeted him with surprise but with delighted cordiality.

But as Robert laid aside his hat he started.

"Good heavens, Saunders!" he said; "you must have been horribly ill. What's up?"

Robert turned. He had not looked in a glass for

two days. One hung near him, and as he turned only an effort kept him from showing his own amazement. The dark brown waving hair was streaked with gray, and the face, lined and haggard with pain, seemed that of a man of fifty.

"I've had a hard pull," he said, "and have come down for a change."

Mitchell looked anxiously at him.

"I should say you were a candidate for the hospital," he said. "Is this the way Barnett turns out his patients? You'd better come home with me to my mother, Saunders. She's heard about you, and she'll be glad to have you. Where are your traps?"

Robert protested, but in the end Mitchell prevailed.

"We dine at six," he said, after the office boy had been dispatched for the valise. "What do you want to do to-day?"

"See life," Robert answered, "I shall simply go about the city till then, and need no guide."

"You're not fit to go alone. I wish I were not tied up to-day," Mitchell said. "To-morrow I am free. Hadn't you better go straight to the house?"

"No," Robert said decisively. "I am much better than I look. This is all new to me. I have never seen a city, you know, and I want to see it all. *All,*" he added significantly. "You promised in July to initiate me if the time ever came when I wanted initiation, and though I did not expect to claim the promise in

September it has come, you see. Are you as ready as I am ?"

"Ready enough," Mitchell said, as Robert looked back from the open door, "but, Saunders, I vow I should as soon show a ghost around. You're not fit to sit up all day, much less all night."

Robert had gone, and Mitchell shook his head as looking from the window he saw him turn into the broad avenue and walk slowly away. There was something in his face which prevented question, and as he returned late in the afternoon interest in the strange life about him seemed to have restored part, at least, of the light and color that had been missing. Mitchell's home was another surprise in its elegance of appointment, but he met the unaccustomed ceremonies with a quietness which astonished the former, and caused his mother—a fashionable and critical woman—to say, "I thought there would be more of the clown about your prodigy, Tom. He must have come of good stock, for though he is raw there is really some distinction about him. You will soon give him a tone."

It was no fault of Mitchell's if, in the fortnight that followed, the missing "tone" did not fully develop itself. Robert went wherever he was led, and learned by personal knowledge what life offers to the gay, reckless, pleasure-loving man of the world, who demands that every sense shall have its special gratification, and who, if the day has brought any overstress of work, makes the night yield its compensation of play. Mitchell had too delicate tastes to care for gross dissipation, but his life when frankly opened out showed such phases as seemed to Robert, even when most tempted to make them his own, the death of all he had come to believe the portion of real manhood. Lockwood's look of strong, cheery hopefulness, Ruth's pure, steady face, continually rose between him and these new distractions, and instead of drowning thought and losing the pressure of obligation to his own soul, he found that no pleasure had such power, and that each day gave him only new perplexity added to the old burden. Believing himself an outcast from the common life of man, and bearing the whole weight of the curse pronounced in his boyhood, faithless, despairing, and with an anguish of longing for the life from which he had fled, he sought to lose himself in the whirl of the city, forget the instincts that had ruled him, lay aside the code under which his life had grown, and be as other men. But with every attempt he recoiled. Gleam as the cup might, through the foam and sparkle the grinning death's head seemed always at the bottom. Life held something better than this, and it was not long before he came to the resolution that though cursed with a curse his soul should bear it as Lockwood bore his burden. A stainless life could be his goal, and should be. If God was, at all, justice would work. If love was denied, at least peace might sometime come, but he would fight the fight steadily, with as little thought of reward as his weakness allowed. Some day the cloud might lift.

One evening he rose from the chair in which he had thrown himself as he closed his door upon Mitchell, stepped to the window, opened it and looked out. Deep night had settled down. He gazed upon the city and its twinkling lights; then to the stars, shining serenely down upon the turmoil and trouble and striving of the myriad lives below them. Again he recalled the movement when the meaning of Searles's words had dawned upon him and he had sprung forward with a passion the memory of which still shook him.

"Mother was right. There is murder in me too," he said, under his breath. "Some day it will work its will in spite of me, and I, too, shall face the same fate that my father knew. My God—if there is a God—*must* I be bound forever in this chain? Is there no help?"

Hot tears came to his eyes. He kneeled by the open window and hid his face. All the old despair and bitterness—the wild protest against fate—rose once more. He stretched out his arms as if the longing that filled him could bring deliverance, and then there was a long silence, the motionless figure giving no sign of the struggling, storm-tossed soul seeking a rest that was nearer than it knew. For quietness came at last. Whether through the mere weariness of conflict or through the strange hush about him he could not tell. Defiance had passed and only longing remained. Once more he lifted his face to the stars, knowing himself defeated, yet with a sense that victory might still come and that through unknown ways he should yet find answer to every question.

"I cannot understand," he said; "I will not even try to understand. I will wait God's will, and live my life as truly as I may."

Again he recalled the words Lockwood had spoken on that last miserable night, "The chain that limits you is a gossamer thread compared to the one that binds me, body and soul, and yet I believe in God,"— and as he recalled them once more a longing went up for a faith that could walk quietly over this dark way and believe that it led not to death but to life. With the longing came a reproach that he could have thus delayed his errand. An over-mastering despair had held him: a stronger impulse now carried him away.

Mrs. Mitchell the next morning in vain urged his longer stay, and begged him if he returned to consider her house his home. Something in him had stirred her motherly feeling, strong under all her worldliness, and as she held his hands for a moment in their good-by, tears came to her eyes and a most unaccustomed "God bless you," to her lips.

"I should like to get at the heart of that thing," Mitchell said to himself, as he parted from Robert at the depot. "There's some sort of tragedy going on. Curious, up in that little mining village! One wouldn't suppose there was life enough there to get up a tragedy; but evidently something has happened."

Robert's journey ended in Vermont the second day. He left the train at St. Albans, and next day took the lumbering old stage running three times a week between there and Lowgate. Now that the end was so nearly reached inward misgiving was strong. But any pain was better than lack of knowledge, and the feeling that his mother's only relatives were here and that some one of his own blood might make him welcome had its comforting side. The driver by whom he sat, a grizzly and weather-beaten man, who had driven the stage full forty years, asked an occasional question, but found small attention in the abstracted passenger, who looked straight ahead and seemed to have no words to spare. He roused himself as they stopped before the post-office, and reflected that twenty years of change had worked here as well as in his own life, and that his errand might be fruitless after all.

"I want to find Silas Mann's house," he said. "Is there such a place in the village?"

"Over there," the driver said, pointing with his whip, and Robert, taking his valise, walked down the street, under great elms whose pale yellow leaves were falling fast, and across to the house, before which stood two stately maples still glowing with autumn color. There was no sign of life in front, and he walked around to the back to find it equally shut up and silent. A window in the next house opened, and a head was put out.

"What do you want?" a sharp voice said.

"I want to find Silas Mann and his wife."

"You'll have to go up to the church-yard, then," the voice said, "they've been there a good fifteen year."

The window went down, but lifted again.

"If you want to know about 'em, go across, three houses up the other side," the voice said. "That's Judge Allen's; an' he knows."

Robert turned away, half determined to go back to St. Albans and cease this vain quest for a knowledge evidently never to come to him in ways of his own choosing; then, shaking off the feeling of discouragement and depression strong upon him, crossed the street once more, passing the old stage-driver, who stood chuckling.

"You might 'a' saved your fare, if you'd been less savin' of your tongue," he said, but Robert only glanced at him, still as if in a dream, and passing on, lifted and dropped the curious brass knocker of the Judge's door, and stood waiting.

CHAPTER XXIII.

TWO hours later the few loungers on the tavern porch saw the stranger cross the street, unlock the door of the old Mann house and close it behind him as he entered. And the same loungers a few moments later saw also that Judge Allen came out and went down the path between his house and Lawyer Denison's, the son of the first executor of Uncle Silas's will.

"You may depend upon't somethin's up," said the stage-driver. "Likely's not somebody's turned up to keep the town out o' that estate, just as the time was pretty nigh out that anybody could claim it. This next April settled it. That feller I brought up had something more'n common on his mind."

"What'll you bet he ain't a fraud?" said a sallow young man, chewing a long straw.

"Fraud or no fraud, Denison'll see through him," the driver said, emphatically. "Between the Jedge and Bob Denison he'll have to make out a pretty good case to get the handlin' o' that property.

"It's a pretty fat sum to have had the handlin' of

fifteen year," he went on after a pause. "If it was any
other men you might say some would stick to their
fingers; but the Jedge can account for every penny
on't. Seventeen odd thousand, and compoundin'
straight ahead for fifteen year. An' then the place.
The house is gone to rack and ruin, to be sure, but
there's the land and the wood-lot. There's a good fifty
thousand if there's a cent; maybe more."

"That ain't much in these days," the tavern-keeper
answered, considerately. "Take your A. T. Stewarts,
now. There's plenty of 'em that'd put away fifty thousand in a vest pocket and think no more about it."

"Well, this fellow don't look as if he'd be certain
what to do with five," the stage-driver said, rising
slowly. "Han'some, but there's somethin' out o' kil-
ter. There'll be news afore night."

And news there was, creeping as news will through
unknown ways. Neither lawyer had told, but by evening every man who joined the group gathered in the
store for their nightly installment of gossip knew that
the heir to the Mann property had been found, and, in
spite of all urging from the Judge and from Miss Priscilla, the Judge's daughter, had gone over to the old
house, followed by Dilly, the black cook, with such
necessities for comfort as could be brought to bear
upon the long-closed rooms, bent upon having his first
night in his own ground in the very room his mother
had known as a girl. To sit quietly under Miss Priscilla's questions or to hear the Judge's explosive

" Pretty Patty Pearsons's boy ! Bless my soul ! I can't believe it ! ' was more than he could bear.

The point of actual legal identification was settled the next morning by the appearance of Captain Rushmore, quite beside himself with delight. Such identification, though unnecessary so far as his acceptance by his mother's old friends was concerned, was essential before any transfer of papers could be made, and Robert had been for a moment utterly at a loss what course to take. Weeks or even months might pass before his mother could be heard from, letters reaching her only through Cranstoun ; but as he sat in perplexed thought the old lake-captain and his retirement to Ogdensburgh occurred to his mind, and at once he telegraphed. The answer was in person, for the down train brought the captain early the next morning, and Miss Priscilla added another stranger to her list of people to be distrusted. Her doubts of Robert were still a source of uneasiness when the cause of his summons had been made known.

" He's unnatural !" she said decisively, on that first night. " Not twenty-one, and gray as a badger. There is something that ain't right. It makes me crawl to see such eyes under that gray hair. They go right through you. I suppose he feels the disgrace."

" What disgrace?" snapped the Judge. " A young fellow like that, with fifty thousand of his own, won't be troubled much with disgrace. That business of the trial was hurried through too quick, Denison always said. He'd been sweet on Patty himself, and he says yet he never saw a woman's face like hers. He shook that boy's hand to-day as if he'd shake it off. I thought he'd cry on the spot. I never was more glad of anything in my life."

"He comes over here a sight to see," pursued Miss Priscilla, ignoring all but her own thought, "with the dust, and what not, in that old house. What do you suppose he'll do with it?"

"Just what we wouldn't look to have him," the Judge answered; and Miss Priscilla swept away indignant, pausing to remark as she passed out:

"I hope he'll see the ghost, or a dozen of 'em."

With the locking of the old door between himself and the prying eyes under which he had winced, Robert felt a burden roll away. Too dazed as yet to take in figures or care for the elaborate papers and accounts Judge Allen brought forward, one thing remained clear: an actual home was his. Not a home where he had been endured, as in the years with his mother, or that other home where his thought of happiness had dwelt, and from which it had vanished in one day, but a home where he could live and work, hide his pain from these strangers, who would never guess it, and make the most of such life as lay before him.

He walked through the old rooms, his lamp casting strange shadows as he went. The people who for a year or two had occupied them had left everything as they found it. Aunt Huldah's straight-backed rocking-chair still stood near the south window, and near it the little table holding the old family Bible. In the square parlor, with its dingy hair-cloth furniture, hung a framed sampler with the name "Huldah Simmons, aged nine. 1781." And above the high mantelpiece was a portrait of Uncle Silas, taken by some traveling painter whose peculiar theories of color and drawing had not had power to destroy a certain life-likeness which showed the possession of a gift only wanting knowledge to ensure good work. Robert looked long at the gentle eyes which twenty years before had watched a sorrow deep or deeper than his own.

"If he had lived," he said, "I should have had a friend, not through affection alone, like Lockwood, but through a tie of blood. Now there is no living soul but mother and Benoni, and she will never think of me as anything but her sorrow and curse. I wonder if there is any one belonging to my father, or if either of these lawyers know. To-morrow I will ask. They won't thank me for looking them up, however. The family disgrace is safely buried, and they will hardly want reminders. No, I am alone, and alone I will remain. It is my fate."

Sad, but quiet, he lay down in the little room that Dilly had made ready with a shiver of fear as she entered it. The ghost walked here, and she had scurried away with one backward glance of terror as a strange, rustling sound echoed through the room. Only the fluttering of loosened paper, but mysterious enough to have grown into a procession of phantoms as she rushed in to report to Miss Priscilla.

Robert slept dreamlessly. Neither rustling, nor the strange creaking and groaning of the old beams, nor the march of myriad rats, pausing in astonishment to survey the presumptuous human who had suddenly invaded their domain, had power to rouse him. He woke at last, refreshed and strong. The weight of yesterday and the many weary days before had lightened. He had a place in the world, and could make it a worthy one.

A white frost glistened on the ground as he walked down the leaf-strewn path to the gate. The air was crisp and keen, but the sunshine lay on the fallen leaves and the sky was blue above him. He bared his head, and looked off to the distant line of mountains, not brown and red, like the copper hills of that other north, but blue and still against the sky. Something of the old pleasure in mere living came to him—a long, full breath, as of a burden lifting. As he stood, the Judge opened his door and looked out, and Robert saw coming toward him Mr. Denison, a quiet, gray-haired man, with keen, watchful eyes, a face of marked New England type, and lit up now with kindliness.

"You're due at Allen's to breakfast," he said, "but after that I want a talk with you. Mary wants to see you, too."

"Mary?" Robert repeated, in a tone of wondering inquiry.

"My girl," the lawyer said. "The only one in a family of six boys. She is just seventeen, and sadly used to her own way. This old house has been our village romance, you know, and you must expect some excitement over the unknown hero who comes riding in to claim his own. Every soul in town will be on the lookout."

"Then I shall leave it, fast as possible," Robert said, a sudden resolution forming. "I have business at Port Henry and shall go up the lake this afternoon. By the time I return the first fever will be over."

"I was going myself to-morrow," the lawyer said, "but if you don't object to society I can make it to-day. The stage leaves in an hour."

Without waiting for answer he hurried on, and Robert obeyed the Judge's beckoning hand, and went in to the waiting breakfast. Miss Priscilla set her lips firmly when told that he would start in an hour, but return in a few days. Why didn't he stay, now he was here, and let them know what his plans were? It looked very suspicious.

"Are you sure he doesn't mean mischief?" she said, as they watched him go over to the stage, passing through a number of interested and curious spectators. "You ought to be pretty sure you ain't mistaken, father."

The Judge laughed and turned aside. Miss Priscilla's faculty for doubt, and her sense that but for her warning voice, this keen, hard-headed father would be hopelessly swamped by his own readiness to accept statements on too limited evidence, struck him always with fresh amusement.

"Keep a sharp lookout, Priscilla," he said, and walked off.

CHAPTER XXIV.

HE lawyer proved a good traveling companion, and beguiled the eight miles' ride with stories of smuggling adventure and the curious life of the country about them. The journey to Burlington was a short one, and they went on board the steamboat a little after noon. The day had grown as warm as early September, and taking chairs on deck after their dinner they settled down for the afternoon.

"I shall leave you just below Port Henry," the lawyer said. "Do you know how to find your way? Remember," he added, as Robert hesitated, "I am an old friend—I may as well tell the truth, an old lover—of your mother's, and it is no fault of mine that I cannot call you son. Anything I could do for my own boy I should gladly do for you."

"There is no need of concealing my errand," Robert said after a few moments of silence. "I want to see for myself the record of my father's trial and go over the ground as thoroughly as possible. Are any of the lawyers living who were on the trial?"

"None that I know of but the Judge himself," Mr.

Denison answered. " He is an old friend of mine. I will give you a letter to him; but are you sure it is best to rake up old memories?"

" Perfectly sure," the young man answered, a little proudly. The boat had started, and the beautiful bay lay before them, down which years ago the mother had sailed, lost to its beauty, her sad eyes seeking only the end of a fruitless journey. The lawyer walked away toward the captain's office and wrote the letter; then climbed to the upper deck and walked up and down as if not certain yet of the wisdom of what was to be done. He stopped by the pilot-house, arrested by the face of the steerer, stood for a few moments watching it keenly, then returned to the office.

" There's something singular about your pilot, Baxter," he said to the captain. " Does he ever drink?"

" Never," said the captain. " There isn't as sober a one on Lake Champlain. He's run with me ten years."

" You'd better take a look at him, nevertheless."

The captain went away grumbling, and returned in a moment triumphant.

" Sober as I am!" he said. " There's something wrong about your own eyes, Denison."

" Very possible," the lawyer said, and returning to Robert, who was walking up and down the deck, the two talked on till the supper bell rang, and they went down to the tables still well filled, though the season proper had ended a month before. Cards were produced as the tables were cleared, and Robert and Denison invited to join. For a few minutes both lingered and watched the game, though neither played. Robert was the first to move.

"It is close here, and I shall walk awhile longer," he said, and returned to the deck now deserted by everyone. The wind blew fresh and chill. He buttoned his overcoat closely about him and walked briskly till he was in a warm glow. The moon was at the full, and they moved now .under the precipitous cliffs on the eastern shore. Far down, a wall of rock seemed to rise, and at the west he could just discern the faint line of the Adirondacks, Mount Marcy towering high among them. The beauty of the night filled him—its peace stole into his soul. These quiet heights piling in the distance, guarding the silent lake, held rest. Under their shadow his father had lived, and on that final day Robert knew that the last words he had been heard to say were :

"I will lift up mine eyes unto the hills, from whence cometh my help."

A felon's death it might have been, but no felon's soul went to meet it.

As they had walked and talked through the afternoon Denison had told the younger man every pleasant thing he could recall of his father's life, and then all the impression, still alive and strong, that Patty had made upon him during her year in the little village; and Robert had listened with the keenest avidity She had loved, then—this silent woman in whom love seemed dead—and her heart was not hard, but buried in the grave with the lover of her youth. A new sense of her life came upon him. He understood her silence. His own pain taught him what pain had been hers. A tenderer feeling than he had ever felt came to him.

"Poor Mother!" he said softly. "Perhaps this new fortune will brighten her life, too."

He looked off to the shore. They were nearing the wall of rock he had noted a few minutes before, and, it seemed to him, heading straight for it. Denison came out through the dim cabin and stood by him; then started.

"There's something wrong," he said. "There's no channel there!"

The captain's voice was heard overhead :

"Stacy! you're mad, man!"

For one awful moment the two stood. Then Denison shouted to the men who had followed him up :

"Back! Back!" and rushed to the other end, pulling Robert with him. But as they ran the shock came, and with a crash that split every timber, and crushed the forward deck and cabin like egg-shells, the boat, with all steam on, plunged at the cliff towering above, and then, held by the rocks below, quivered as if a moment more would send to the bottom what remained.

After the first terrified shock the few women were quiet, hushing the screaming children. The captain ordered back the frightened deck hands and hurried the passengers forward, aiding them to the shelf of rock.

"For your lives!" he shouted. "She'll go down in three minutes."

In less than that time everyone on board had found footing, and the captain himself helped to lift the only injured one, a Canadian fireman, who had tried to jump and been crushed between boat and rock. It had all come and gone like an evil dream. Even as they turned to see the peril from which every soul had escaped, with one lurch the vessel was gone, and in a moment only a swirl in the moonlit water showed what their fate might have been.

"Let us give thanks to our Lord God," said a passenger—a gray-haired man—falling on his knees, and in broken words seeking to speak the gratitude for life, and then with the others he joined in making the women as comfortable as possible. The rock was less steep than it had looked. It was possible to climb to the summit, and the space where they were, though narrow, afforded ample foothold, but that was all. Above them, accessible by a narrow way which must at some time have been used, it was soon found that the rock shelved back, overhung from above, and forming, if not a cave, at least a protection against the frost and wind. One by one the party ascended. Brush was gathered and a fire lighted, over which the shivering women and children hovered, and soon from the other side an answering blaze showed that friends were on the way.

"Keep your spirits up," the captain said, though his

pale face showed his own distress over the unaccountable catastrophe. "It's one of the Port Henry tugs. You'll have breakfast at Port Henry, every one of you."

"Every one but Stacy," the first mate said. "Did you know he hadn't turned up, captain?"

"He'd be strung up where he stood if he did," the captain said between his teeth. "It's the work of a madman. Every soul of us might have been at the bottom. I've run on the lake forty year, boy and man, and never saw nor heard of such a piece of work."

"Did you see him?" a voice asked.

"Just one minute and no more," the captain said. "I went to the upper deck and saw we were far out of the channel, and ran forward. Stacy stood there with his eyes set and as unconscious as a dead man. I caught the wheel and gave one turn backward, but it was too late. I saw him spring over, and ran back, and then came the crash. Drunk, I suppose; but he's at the bottom somewhere, and we're never likely to know."

"He swims like a duck," the mate said. "He may have come up somewhere and got ashore. I've seen him sit that same sort of way, and never answer, but I don't believe it was drink. There was no smell of drink, and he had no look of a drinking man. And as to what's happened, I can't believe it now. Half an hour ago a good boat under our feet—I knew every plank in her—and now cast away here with nothing but our lives. It's a miracle there's no more hurt. Have you looked at Baptiste since they laid him down?"

"No," the captain said, starting, "I'd clean forgotten the poor soul. How is he?"

"Going fast, Captain, I think," a voice said. "We put our coats together for a bed, and did what we could, but life's pretty nearly out of him."

Captain Baxter turned, and Robert followed a step or two to the niche where the dying man had been laid. A sudden blaze shot up as some one dropped fresh hemlock boughs upon the fire, and Robert leaned over the maimed body of the poor fellow, who opened his eyes and murmured :

"A priest! Oh, for God's love, a priest. Is there no one here?"

His look wandered from one to another, then fell upon Robert. He rose suddenly and with staring, horror-stricken eyes cried out—a cry so full of deadly terror that the listeners shivered in hearing and the children burst into crying again—

"Robert Saunders! Robert Saunders! For the love of God leave me. Take him away! Take him away!"

He fell back, covering his eyes with his hands, but crying still,

"Take him away!"

Robert bent over him.

"I am Robert Saunders, truly," he said, "but how can you know it?"

"He's out of his head," one of the men said. "Baptiste, you never saw him before."

"I saw him go to his death," the man cried, putting

out his hands. "I sent him there. Holy Mother of God! I did the murder, and he was innocent. Oh, for a priest!"

As if light from Heaven itself had suddenly gleamed upon the past, Robert saw what must be. The stained memory of an innocent man might be cleansed, and the guilt-burdened soul of the dying culprit would be lightened by the confession, made before God and to his fellow men, even if not received by the authorized officers of law or religion. The dying man still turned in terror away, but Robert, quivering with excitement, held his place.

"Come quickly," he called to Denison, who stood feeding the fire. "Here is a confession you must hear. Quick! There is no time to lose."

Denison came forward hastily. Robert's face was set and stern, but the light of some new hope was in it.

"Quick!" he said again. The dying man looked up once more. Whether Denison's pale, thin face, and coat buttoned to his chin in the chill night air, conveyed to the sinking man some sense of a priestly presence, none could say; nor was there any question. The man spoke instantly, eagerly, and so clearly that all about heard.

"He wasn't dead. I saw them fight. I saw Saunders drag him under the brush and go. I saw he had taken nothing. I saw there was money. I went only to get the money. Not to kill—holy Mother of God!—not to kill. He stirred when I took his watch. Then I choked him till he lay still, and covered him again. I would have told. I did not want to hurt Robert Saunders, but I was afraid. I hated Crandall, for he had done me a bad turn. I was glad he was dead."

Although for one moment utterly confounded, Denison's quick instinct told him what was needed, and taking out his note book he wrote swiftly as the broken words followed one another, adding as the voice ceased:

"I, Baptiste Leroy, confess that I am the murderer of Thomas Crandall, and that Robert Saunders was innocent of the crime for which he was hung."

"He can't write," the captain said.

"He can make his mark," Denison answered. The men raised him, and Robert steadied the stiffening hand as the mark was made, hardly visible in the flickering, uncertain light—but *there !*

"Absolution !" he muttered, but even with the word fell back, cringing, from the form he still believed to be the accusing spirit of the man he had sinned against. Once more he cried, "Absolution !" And, even with the word, the spirit passed into the presence of the Judge—and the Father—of all the earth.

Robert sat down by the lifeless body and buried his face. He could neither think nor feel. The men fell back and left him to himself. Denison stood silent for a moment, then returned to the curious group about the fire, deeming it best to answer all questions then and there. The captain sat as if stunned. He had known Robert's father, and been one of the party who watched with Searles in the attempt to break the Sandy Hill jail and rescue him.

"I said then I'd give all I had in the world to settle the thing," he said at last, "but I never thought that twenty years afterward I'd be taken at my word, and my boat go to the bottom to get at the rights of it. Where's the boy?"

"Let him alone," Denison said. "He has had all he can bear."

"Here's a let-up for all of us," the mate said. "The tug's in sight; two of 'em!"

In a moment all heard the sound of wheels and the puff of steam, which told that the strange night had ended and a new day begun. From the very gate of death full life had sprung, and as Robert took his place on the little tug, and listened to the wonder and dismay of the rescuers, no room was left in his soul for sense of loss, or terror at the danger he had passed.

"Never any more a curse," sounded over and over in his soul, as if these were the only words brain could hear or heart desire, and as at last morning and sunshine came again, and he walked up the village street that Patty's sad steps had trodden twenty years before, the burden of his life rolled away, and with bowed head and soul full of solemn joy one thought went up:

"I believe in God."

CHAPTER XXV.

EN days later Patty sat by the open fire in the low room. It was unchanged in any respect since the days when Robert, stretched on the bear-skin before it, read by the flickering light, or followed the flame as it darted up the wide chimney. Cæsar, grown older and heavier, but still alert and keen, lay in his old place at the feet of Benoni, who sat busily repairing some snares. Patty's knitting had fallen from her hands. Her eyes were bent on the glowing coals, the look of long pain, silently borne, still in them. Again, as she looked, the weary years seemed to pass one by one in slow procession; the old home, the level grave under the swaying birch-tree, the long journey, and then the making of this new home, always, day by day, with its reminder of that other one. She saw the laughing dark eyes and beautiful head of the baby, grasping Benoni's finger, clutching Cæsar as he stood patient and submissive, the busy feet seeking always some new way to walk in, the little hands she had put away resolutely from the clinging clasp that learned at last to spend itself on the silent uncle. She saw again the look of bewilderment and pain in the child's face in the conflict which had been the seal of her own resolution—the indifference of boyhood, which stabbed her, even when surest that it was her own work, and best so. The sharp longing, as sharply put down, for the love she would never know. Then the fierce outbreak —the storm which had driven them asunder, and the silent years in which she had waited for the end.

It must come, and before her own life had passed. The cup would not be full till her own eyes had seen the evil in store—her own lips once more tasted the bitter draught of another's sin. Beyond this all was dark. If only the crime and punishment, which she foresaw as inevitable for this inheritor of the hard promise, proved expiation for the past, and in Robert the curse might end! For this day by day she prayed, and her hands clasped and her lips moved now in the anguish of entreaty :

"How long, O Lord? How long?"

Cæsar stirred uneasily and lifted his head; then gave a low bark and shook himself as he arose. Benoni looked up also—the mysterious inward sense, the equivalent of hearing, warning him of the sound to which his outward ears were dead. In these years their own immediate surroundings had altered but little, though ten miles back from the lake a small settlement had cleared ground and opened up the rich land for cultivation, and now and then, after a day's fishing on the lake, some one from it sought shelter in this—the only house for miles. Benoni rose and opened the door as a light knock was heard. Cæsar growled low, then looked up, snuffed eagerly, and with one bound and a sound compounded of bark and howl of joy planted his great feet on the stranger's shoulders.

"Down, Cæsar," Patty said, starting forward; for the dog was fierce, and such demonstration strange and unusual; but Cæsar, though dropping to the ground, whirled about in an ecstasy of delight, barking with such tremendous power that speech was useless.

"Quiet, Cæsar," said the stranger imperatively, and Patty stood motionless. The voice she knew; but as the tall figure moved a step forward, and removing the hat showed hair thickly sown with gray, she looked from the dark eyes, surely Robert's, to the face, still bearing marks of the hard conflict out of which it had come; young still, but with the brightness of something more than youth as he looked at her with a look she could not interpret. Love, surely! And her heart leaped to meet the demand, silent since his babyhood.

"Robert?" she said faintly, putting out her hands. Then they fell. The spell of years was still upon her. "Is it Robert?"

"Yes, it is Robert," he said, taking her hand and looking at her wistfully. Benoni stood near, holding him fast, and tears running down his face as he passed his hand over the gray head and made the sign denoting heavy sickness. "I have come to tell you something, Mother. I have strange news; and I have journeyed far since I was able to tell it."

Patty looked at him, still silent, but her eyes widening with dread of what she might hear. Sorrow had come, and sin, it must be, too; else why the worn face and white locks on the head that for a moment she had longed to clasp to her bosom and bless? Yet the face held peace and light: a look that had been on his father's face that morning long ago as she unclasped her arms and left him forever. She bent forward eagerly. Her breath came quick and hard. Perhaps —perhaps out of the sin redemption had come to the son, though for the father it had not been possible. Robert caught her as for a moment she tottered, and placed her in her chair.

"It is good news," he said. "The only news in the world that could be good for either you or me. Mother, for twenty-one years you have believed a lie. My father died an innocent man. He was no murderer, and here are all the papers that prove my words."

Patty looked at him in terror, then burst into a passion of weeping and clasped him to her.

"Oh, my boy, my boy!" she cried. "This is the way it has had to end. And I thought for a minute there could be good for either of us! God has taken your senses. You are mad, and so the curse has worked!"

"Hush, Mother," Robert said, as she clung to him. "I wish I could have told you differently. Try and be quiet, and understand. I have not lost my senses. I have been at Lowgate, to Uncle Silas's house. I have talked with Thomas Denison and Judge Allen. You remember them both. This paper is the Judge's own cancelling of the sentence he passed upon my father. There is everything here needed to clear his name and ours. Try and listen, and I will tell you the whole."

Patty sat down, trembling still, but trying to be calm. If this were delusion it would soon prove itself, and the old names held a soothing power in themselves. Her eyes were fastened on Robert's face as he spoke, and they never moved as the story went on. He told it from the beginning. His own pain—the burden she had put upon him, and the burden it had remained, till at last it had seemed to lighten and he had come to hope in a future. A quiver went over her as he spoke of Searles, and her hands clasped tight as he spoke of the last days at Houghton and the shock of discovery. Detail by detail, till the last words were spoken, and he had read the formal phrases of the affidavits which held Baptiste Leroy's confession—the paper given by the Judge—everything that had been deemed necessary to convince her of the full truth.

"And now, Mother," he said, at last, as he laid the package on her knee, that she might see for herself, if inclined, "now your banishment is over. You owe it to my father's memory to go back to his people and and yours—the people who knew you both. I have stayed long enough to arrange for it all. You must go away from here, and at once. The old house is waiting for you. I have done nothing to it because I knew you would like best to settle it after your own mind, and you and Benoni must go back with me. That is my first work—and then——."

Patty rose slowly, and stretched out her hands as if in the dark feeling her way. Robert looked at her in alarm as she strove vainly to speak. Her face worked strangely—she gasped for breath, then fell before him and held his knees. .

"Forgive me! forgive me!" she prayed, and tears came again in floods. "I shall never be forgiven in this world or the next. Oh, my God, *why* could I not have known!"

"Hush, Mother," Robert said again, his arms around her and his hands pressing the poor head to his cheek. "There is nothing to forgive. You thought you were right, and I know how you suffered. I never could have known but for just such pain in my own soul. I went through the depths. I was faithless and hopeless, and out of it all my God has led me—the God you did not believe in enough to trust his love, but who is, for both of us, our portion forever. Hush, hush, dear Mother!"

Then, after a pause, rightly judging that care for his wants would be a relief to her from the intense emotion of the last hour, he added: "When you are better you must give me supper, Mother. I have walked over from the new village. I had not forgotten one turn of the woods, though so much is changed. Now, while you are busy, let me tell Benoni."

Patty rose. Robert had dreaded the self-reproach which might be the reaction of these silent years, and determined on swift measures to set it aside, and in the strong pressure of his warm young arms Patty, as he lifted her from the floor and smiled his old bright smile, felt that not only forgiveness but love was there, and pressed his lips with the first mother's-kiss they had ever known.

"God bless my son—the son who has everything to forgive, and who does forgive his mother!" she said solemnly. Benoni bent over her as she lifted her head. Little as he yet understood, he knew well that a new life had begun, and kissed her cheek with the old affection which for years had had no outward token. Then Robert, holding his hand, made it all plain to him also, Cæsar sitting with head on his knee, and eyes running over with love that eyes only could speak.

Patty prepared coffee, and brought out venison that Benoni had killed, and Robert ate and drank with the eagerness of a hungry boy; Patty's pale face lighting with a smile as she watched him.

"Now to bed," he said, "and to-morrow we'll settle things. No, my own place," he added, as she motioned toward her own room. "I could not sleep anywhere else." He mounted the narrow stair to the little room which he had never thought to see again. Once more he lay down in the bed on which he had tossed in that last night of misery, and once more looked out to the same stars that had shone on the sad, bitter conflict alone. To night they saw only peace—peace, and a longing for another good toward which his heart leaped, but for which he could well wait a little longer. Patty came softly up the stair and bent over him.

"Is it comfortable?" she said. "Can you sleep in such a little place?"

Robert drew her down to him, and she kissed him passionately.

"How can you love me?" she said with tears. "I had almost ruined your life. My own is ruined."

"Never," Robert said. "There are good days for both of us. Go now to rest, Mother, for you need it, and I want you to be strong. Good night."

"Good night, my son," she said softly, still holding to him as if she could not let go—then, left him.

CHAPTER XXVI.

ROBERT had dreaded the morning, fearing what the night might bring of sadness or self-accusation; but to his surprise all this seemed to have been lost in the flood of gratitude which overwhelmed Patty. Far into the night she had lain, going over, as if in a dream, the years which held now no bitter memory, no hopeless outlook, but a sure promise that the sundered lives would meet in the eternity to come. She slept at last, and in dreams saw once more the lover of her youth, standing afar off, yet with that look of light and peace that she had never forgotten, though remembering it with a dull pain that it should have been his delusion and almost hers. Now, she strove to reach him and could not; yet the face seemed nearer, and a great love filled it.

"Robert! Oh my Robert," she cried, stretching out her arms. Daylight had come, and as she rose up, her long hair falling about her and her face alight with love and longing, Robert's son bent over her, and in his face she saw the same look, the same promise.

"I was dreaming," she said, a faint color coming

231

to her face as she fell back; but Robert as he left her saw that the old look was gone, and that at last had come the "clear shining after rain."

Patty's face could never be anything but quiet and steady, but pain and hardness had gone. In their stead was an almost beseeching humility. She followed Robert with hungry eyes. Nature and habit hindered demonstration, but the feeling of the night before had had its way and broken down every hindrance. To-day it lay, no longer a shut-in, hidden stream, but a deep still source, open to air and sun shine, and filling her life henceforward with sweet waters. There would be few words, but Robert knew at last that mother-love was his own, and would be to the end.

Within a day or two all needed preparations were made for the journey down to the first railroad station. Robert had provided a dress less antiquated than her usual one, and Patty wore it with a pride in his thoughtfulness and a confidence in the wisdom of his selection that moved him curiously. It was a widow's dress, and her clear-cut, beautiful face looked out from the close, black bonnet with a new hope—a quietness—that made many turn to look as the journey went on.

Mary Denison, whom Robert had met on his return from the lake, had entered into his plans with all a girl's enthusiasm; and Miss Priscilla's sense of the fitness of things received the keenest outrage that all these unprecedented experiences had yet given it on learning that Mary had had money put in her hands for all necessary expenses, and, without disturbing the general arrangement, was to have the old place in as perfect order as could be, with the decay and wear of time. An aunt of Mary's, who had known Patty in her youth, aided her in restoring the rooms to their former look.

And so, when, one chill November afternoon, the stage left at the door the three figures for whom the old house was waiting, Patty, as she entered the once familiar rooms, felt that at last she had come home. A day later Robert went with her to the little church-yard.

"I could not leave him by the lake," he had said, "and I knew this would be your home, rather than the old one. So he is here, by Uncle Silas and Aunt Huldah, and I have planted another birch that will not need long to grow and shadow them all."

Patty looked silently at the familiar names on the two weather-stained stones—then turned to the other —a plain granite shaft, on which were the words:

ROBERT NELSON SAUNDERS,

BORN, JULY 15TH, 18—,
DIED, AUGUST 3D, 18—,

"I cried unto the Lord, and he heard, and delivered me from all my trouble."

"He has delivered us," she said, slow tears falling over her cheeks, but a smile on her lips. "Now, Robert, you must go. You have done nothing for yourself, and everything for me."

"Then you are quite willing, Mother?" Robert said. "You will never have any more feeling about it?"

"It is my atonement," Patty said solemnly. "I don't know, Robert, that I could be willing if it were not for that. But now I am, and you may tell Benjamin Searles that, if my rash words have made his burden too heavy in these years, I take them back. To give him my son is the hardest thing I could do, but he may take it as a sign that there is a better life for all of us."

"I may come back to you to be taken care of, after all," Robert said, as they turned away. "How do I know that Ruth will be as willing as her father?"

"You will not come back," Patty said quietly; and in his heart Robert knew it must be so. Together, this last evening, they talked over what he would do, Benoni and Cæsar again sitting by. Robert had arranged matters so that a fixed income would be paid his mother, more than sufficient with her own property for her simple wants, and planned now, when he had made the journey once more, to possibly enter the School of Mines at Yale, and fit himself more thoroughly for his work. Work and the future lay in the West and not the East. He had grown up there and knew its life. Every interest centered about the little town where his real life had begun. Lowgate should count as the old homestead. to which from year to year

he would return, he and Ruth, and perhaps——
Robert's heart thrilled as he added, deep in his soul,
"the children, on whom no curse will lie, but only a
blessing."

So at last he turned his face westward, and sped on
to "the haven where he would be," and Patty, sad, yet
with a deep and quiet thankfulness, took up the new
life, into which she fell naturally, even happily, as
though the years that were past were shadows only,
and the true years had just begun. Silent, for nature
and those years had made her so, and with a look of
expectancy always in her eyes, as she awaited the coming of that day for which she longed; but with a face
that children came to love, and that the sick and dying
prayed to have near them—the face of one who had
known all sorrow, and who waited now in those quiet
border-lands for the sunrise and the morning.

Robert had sent a line to Lockwood telling of his
speedy coming, but none to Ruth. It was impossible
to write her; he must wait for speech. But to Ruth
the silence meant only new confirmation of the thought
she had forced in upon herself two months before. She
loved him. He had cared for her. Of that she was certain, but this black shadow lay too heavily between
ever to lift in this world. Their lives were apart. She
dreaded this meeting, and yet longed for it. She would
guard herself so that no thought of her pain could ever
reach him. Perhaps they could be friends; and yet,
how could they? At times she resolved to go away, and

run no chance of losing her own self-control, or giving
him more pain; and then, to go and give up this last
look seemed impossible. So she wavered, doubtful
and troubled, each day a little paler, a little thinner,
and taxing all Miss Tempy's faith and patience as she
looked at her.

Miss Tempy's own waiting time had not been altogether uneventful. There had been one day in which
her cheeks glowed with even more than their usual
color, and her eyes snapped fiercely as she marched
from one household task to another, an occasional
"Well, I never!" escaping under her breath and, as it
were, quite beyond her own volition. At each occur-
rence of this sort she turned sharply upon Ruth, as if
to make her responsible, but finding herself apparently
unobserved went on with the same mysterious energy.
As night approached she was most evidently watching
for something, starting nervously at each step that
seemed to pause near the house, and, when at last the
bell rang, making her escape frantically up the back
stairs.

"Something's wrong with Tempy," Searles said to
Ruth, as she came in with Mr. Brown. "She's never
been in such a way since she came to us. She used to
have tantrums in old times, but I can't see what has
set her off now."

"I don't believe she's well," Ruth said. "Her face
was flushed all day, but she hates to have anybody
ask how she feels."

Ruth looked up and met Mr. Brown's eyes, which had so peculiar an expression that her own were fastened upon him for a moment with intense surprise. Why should he blush so furiously, and what had she said that should bring that extraordinary look, compounded of shyness, a desire to laugh and a certain triumph? It was gone in a moment, and taking his usual place he talked quietly for a time, rising at last and looking toward the door as if he had expected to see Miss Tempy appear.

"Ruth," he said, "I've a message for Miss Perkins. Will you give it, exactly?"

"Surely," Ruth said in surprise.

"Tell her then—" The minister hesitated, then added abruptly, "Tell her I am certain it isn't 'leavings.'"

"'Certain it isn't leavings,'" Ruth repeated mechanically; but Mr. Brown had disappeared even as she spoke. Searles and Lockwood both burst into a laugh, and Ruth, to whom a new idea had come, ran up stairs to Miss Tempy's door.

"I've a message for you," she called.

"Don't want it," came a muffled voice, as if from a face buried in a pillow.

"But, Aunt Tempy, I promised to give it."

"Well, I didn't promise to take it," came the sudden answer. "Go to bed, Ruth. It's time."

"It's only eight o'clock, Aunt Tempy, and all your stockings on the table, and Mr. Brown says, 'Tell her

I'm certain it isn't leavings'—whatever he may mean by that!"

No answer, and Ruth after a moment turned away, when suddenly Miss Tempy's door was flung open, and Ruth pulled in and set down energetically upon a low stool she often occupied. Evidently Aunt Tempy had been crying, but as Ruth looked at her now an almost imperceptible smile struggled to the surface and was instantly repressed.

"Ruth Searles, how dare you bring trifling messages from that old idiot? Don't you ever take another, or give it either. Oh Ruth, Ruth!" and for the first time in the young girl's knowledge Miss Tempy sat down and cried heartily.

"There!" she said, presently, "I'm a worse idiot myself. Whatever you think, Ruth, just be quiet. There's time enough for everything, and till Robert comes back not a word more will I say. What I let you in for is more'n *I* know, and now I'll just let you out, and that's the end of it."

She pushed Ruth away as the girl put one hand on her shoulder, and shut the door decisively, and Ruth, who had forgotten for a little her own heavy heartedness, turned with a sigh to her own room.

CHAPTER XXVII.

WO months had brought no visible change to the little village, and yet a revolution had taken place. Only in one mind, it is true, but sufficient to alter the course of events for many. And like most revolutions, recorded or unrecorded, the apparent cause for final outbreak had been very insignificant in character. Bridget Doylan, who for three years had kept house for "the minister"— Mr. Brown owning and answering to that title as exclusively as if no other could ever claim it—had left her clothes in the tub one Monday morning, returning to them an hour thereafter no longer Bridget Doylan, but Bridget Maguire, to rinse and boil and hang out with her usual composure.

Two hours later excited voices drew Mr. Brown from his study. Bridget stood at bay near the boiler, while near her a tall Irishman, with a watchful eye on the long dipper she held, stood talking eagerly.

"You're a desayvin' villin!" said Bridget.

"An' I'm not," returned Patrick. "Is it desayvin' to ask for the company o' me own wife that I'm not willin' to live widout? Didn't I walk home beyant,

thrue to me word, and give a look into me house, that
lonely I couldn't stand the sight of it, but come
shthraight for the only one that's got a right there?
Biddy, me darlint, ye won't have the heart to say ye
won't be goin' back wid' me?''

"An' I will, thin," returned Bridget. "Whin I
only married you to get rid o' your urgin', niver
dhramin' you'd be comin' this way—an' you promisin'
me all should go on the same."

"Thin I'll have to be callin' in Molly O'Hara agin,"
said Patrick, in tones of deepest dejection, but with a
furtive look at Bridget. "An' I'm that sick of her
simperin' way, an' the foolishness of her, an' she always
a cryin' out, 'Oh, Mr. Maguire, an' shure its moighty
lonesome for ye! Call to me whiniver you loike, to
do the bits o' things you nade.' Didn't I know she
was just waitin' for a word, and wasn't me word an'
heart too all beshpoke?''

"Go away wid the tongue o' yees," said Bridget,
visibly faltering.

"It's a good morning's work, and you may as well
finish as you have begun," now put in Mr. Brown,
quietly. "I didn't suppose you'd steal a march on me
this way, Bridget."

Bridget melted into tears.

"I'd no thought o' lavin'!" she cried.

"But you must," said Mr. Brown. "I can't be the
means of separating husband and wife. Pack your
things, Bridget, and let Pat take them."

"That I'll not," said Bridget, drying her hands and turning on both. "That I'll not, till the washin' an' ironin's out o' the way and the house settled-like. An' I'll come, times, an' see how things is, an' do what I can to keep 'em straight."

Excellent as Bridget's intentions were, time failed to fulfill them. Patrick proved to be an exacting husband, and the four little orphan Maguires gave her more than all the occupation necessary to each day. The ladies of the society came to the rescue, and Mr. Brown grew daily more desperate. When it was not Miss Popples with lemon-pies and her best bonnet, who appeared "just to see what must be done," it was Miss Huggins or Miss Anderson, or some other member of the sisterhood who, since the death of the first Mrs. Brown, had resolved steadfastly to be the second. Mr. Brown took his meals at the hotel, locked his study-door, and avoided the quartette who took turns in dusting his parlor and spoiling his digestion with the latest inventions in cake. Not insensible to his own value, he was still an essentially modest and humble-minded man, who through a varying career had been gentle to all women and eager to avoid offense, till at last, desperate with annoyance, he determined upon summary measures.

One secret nook in his heart the minister reserved for a tender memory—a look, and the warm touch of two little hands that he had hoped to hold in his own at will. But with the knowledge that such hope was vain, practicality had asserted itself, and he saw the dream vanish out of his life. Left to himself, Mr. Brown would have gone on to the end content with his daily round; but Bridget's defection and the sudden onslaught upon his peace were strongest reminders that the parsonage needed an energetic mistress.

And now, who should such mistress be ? Among the various candidates, widowed or maiden, Mr. Brown's fancy roamed, finding some insuperable objection to each, till one evening on his way from the post-office he encountered Miss Tempy returning from the Dorcas meeting and bearing a huge bundle of work. The two were the best of friends. There was a business-like quality in Miss Tempy's walk and conversation that effectually shut off all thought of sentiment, and her excess of energy gave always the impression that she had no time for nonsense of any description. With keenest common-sense and equally keen humor, she and the jolly minister had been comrades from the first, and he recognized her as one of the strongest auxiliaries in his own work. Under the brisk speech and action, and showing itself but thinly veiled behind the keen, black eyes, was hidden a very loyal and generous nature, but never till this morning had it entered Mr. Brown's mind that here was his city of refuge.

Miss Tempy stopped for a moment to pin her shawl afresh, and the moonlight fell full upon her face.

"She is n't bad-looking !" Mr. Brown remarked to

himself with considerable surprise. "In fact, I think she is very good-looking. Strange it never occurred to me before!"

Miss Tempy's curls were sprinkled with gray, and the kindly color seemed to soften the sharp black eyes and the ruddy cheeks. Tall and vigorous, and still owning that rare possession of American middle-age, a set of firm, white teeth, her hearty, unconscious smile as she looked up ended any possible question.

"Miss Tempy," Mr. Brown said; and to his own surprise an unaccountable trepidation took possession of him, "Miss Tempy, I have a suggestion to make. Will you listen to me?"

"I don't know anything to hinder," said Miss Tempy, tranquilly.

"I'm obliged—" said Mr. Brown, "in fact—I've got to make a new arrangement, and I have thought perhaps you would be willing to oversee my house-keeping."

"Lawful heart! do you think I can run two houses?" returned Miss Tempy.

"I think you could run ten if it were necessary, but I only want you to attend to one. Miss Tempy, will you be my wife?"

"A joke's a joke," said Miss Tempy with dignity, "but this is going too far, sir. I'm ashamed of you, Mr. Brown."

"You've no call to be," said the minister unabashed. "I'm in earnest. I don't pretend to any great excitement. I simply ask you, as an honest man who means to make you happy and will try to, to marry me and try it. I think we can have much comfort together."

"Comfort ain't all," said Miss Tempy, turning suddenly upon him and speaking with such energy that the minister fell back a step. "I've my own notions about such things, and I'll never marry a man that takes me because he wants things kept straight. I won't say it isn't a temptation, but the more shame to you, Thomas Brown. I've eyes, and a mind too. Go home, and don't ask me to put up with *leavings*, now or anytime."

With a sudden rush Miss Tempy was gone, and Mr. Brown, somewhat disconcerted, but confident it would end as he wished, walked on. But the word "leavings" held too many suggestions. Did she object to him as a widower, or had she suspected more than he thought of his feeling toward Ruth? In any case he owed her full confession of his weakness, and could trust her discretion, even if she refused to listen for herself. Mr. Brown found himself becoming anxious lest this might be the case, and accordingly the next evening left his message with Ruth; but a week passed before he found it possible to see Miss Tempy alone. Six days longer of siege had made him resolutely bent upon accomplishing his purpose, and his arguments proved effectual.

"Not a thing shall be done till Robert comes," Miss Tempy said, when at last a favorable answer had been obtained. "There sha'n't be goings-on of any sort till that thing's all settled."

"All right," Mr. Brown said, cheerfully. "That will soon be. I sha'n't have to wait long."

If a bomb-shell had suddenly fallen in the main street of Houghton there could not have been profounder amazement than at the announcement made instantly and everywhere by Mr. Brown of his intentions. But, as a whole, the town approved, pronouncing it the most suitable thing he could have done, and Miss Tempy, very heartily in love, became so different a person that Mr. Brown daily congratulated himself upon his astuteness and wondered at his own good luck. He flushed a little when Ruth gave her congratulations, but her frank kindliness soon restored his equanimity. So the days ran on, and again winter was near—and the lake closing fast.

One evening all were away. The steamer, on its last trip, had stopped that afternoon, leaving no passengers. It was possible that Robert would come in one of the Company's propellers, but when was uncertain.

A pile of work lay by her on the table, and an open book—an old fashion of Ruth's, who, forced to learn to sew, solaced herself by bits of rhyme, and had learned many a poem, line by line, between the stitches. The lines before her were not words such as a girl of seventeen often reads or even understands, and to Ruth herself, two months before, they would have held small meaning compared to that which filled them now. But in spite of distance, and inevitable separation, and the long years that must lie between them, ever widening the gulf she must not seek to pass, the words were true, and her quiet voice rose clear and sweet as she repeated the wonderful words of the master-poet:

> " Let me not to the marriage of true minds
> Admit impediment. Love is not love
> Which alters when it alteration finds,
> Or bends with the remover to remove.
> Oh no; it is an ever fixèd mark,
> That looks on tempests and is never shaken;
> It is the star to every wandering bark
> Whose worth's unknown, although his height be taken.
> Love's not Time's fool, though rosy lips and cheeks
> Within his bending sickle's compass come.
> Love alters not with his brief hours and weeks,
> But bears it out even to the edge of doom."

Her voice broke. Her head drooped on the table before her. The door opened softly, but she did not stir. As in a dream she heard a voice say, "Ruth," and as in a dream she lifted her head and looked with wide eyes and parted lips at the figure in the doorway. Then the arms stretched forth. An irresistible force drew her.

"No—no!" she said, hiding her face; but, as she spoke, the arms were about her. She struggled away but they held her fast.

"Ruth," the voice said, "I went away because I thought I must. I have come back for my wife. Shall I have her?"

Three days later the Rev. Mr. Gray was called to the Searles's house, with the injunction to bring his surplice, and on his arrival was met by Miss Tempy, business-like as ever.

"It's ridiculous, I know," she said, "an' I've stood out against it all I can, but Mr. Brown won't hear 'No,' and I can't go off an' leave Ruth a young girl all alone in the house. I know the town'll talk, but it's got to, and you're to marry the whole of us, Mr. Gray ;" with which ambiguous remark Miss Tempy turned to the parlor and took her place composedly, while Ruth, with pale face, but shining, joyful eyes, came forward with Robert.

Is this the end? No, the beginning. The end for us; but, to the two lives that then and there knew that henceforward they could be but one, only the beginning of that story without an end which every happy home may hold. Life they knew might bring sorrow, pain, disappointment; but life it would remain; and death was powerless against a force that, strengthened and rooted in years of tenderness, of gentle offices, of unclouded understanding, would be transplanted to the other life, so that there still the two were one, and Love, in death and life alike, triumphant.

Once more, and for the last time—after years of quiet happiness had made the past sorrow only a shadow—they went to the old home in the mountains.

Children had come, and summer after summer as they grew older had learned to call Robert's inheritance, "Going home to Grandmother's." "Uncle Dwight" was often with them, and found in Robert's life fulfillment of the hopes denied his own. Patty lived again in these children, and, as she watched their fresh, eager life, learned strange lessons she had never dreamed of. Then came a winter when Mary Denison wrote of the mother's failing health; and then a sudden summons. Robert and Ruth traveled night and day, reaching Lowgate one chill spring evening, and entering noiselessly but hastily.

"Just in time," the doctor said, as he came forward. "She has kept alive for you."

Robert bent over her. Patty lay quiet—no motion or breath visible to show if life remained; but as he kissed the still face she opened her eyes and smiled—the old, rare, beautiful smile.

"God bless my son," she whispered, as her hand sought faintly to touch his. Then a change came. Her eyes opened full and clear. She rose suddenly, and her own lovely smile lighted the face to which, for one fleeting moment, life and youth had come back. She stretched out her arms.

"Oh, my love! my love!" she cried. "Robert! You are there! I am coming!"

Words and life died away together. She fell back, but the smile remained, and when the coffin lid closed over her the radiant look still lingered.

Side by side the two lie at last. The birch is a stately tree. The children are children no longer. For Robert and Ruth the shadows lengthen toward the West, but human love and God's love hold, and will hold, not alone to the third and fourth, but to *all* generations.

THE END.

Lightning Source UK Ltd.
Milton Keynes UK
UKOW052◼10270313

20830€UK00007B/197/P